TOGETHER IN OUR DIFFERENCES

HOW NEWCOMERS AND ESTABLISHED RESIDENTS ARE REBUILDING AMERICAN COMMUNITIES

FINDINGS FROM THE COMMUNITY INNOVATIONS PROJECT

Written by:
Julia Teresa Quiroz
Director, Special Projects Division

THE NATIONAL IMMIGRATION FORUM
220 I Street, NE
Suite 220
Washington, DC 20002

January 1995

ISBN 0-9645220-0-4
Copyright © 1995 National Immigration Forum

The National Immigration Forum
220 I Street, NE
Suite 220
Washington, DC 20002

Printed in the United States of America
on recycled paper with soy-based ink.

ACKNOWLEDGMENTS

This report simply would not exist without the support of many wonderful people. I beg my readers to indulge my sentimentality in thanking:

Helene Lauffer, Chair of the Forum Board's Race and Ethnic Relations Task Force, for coming up with the idea in the first place, and providing me with invaluable support and suggestions; all the members of project's **Advisory Committee**, for sharing their time and expertise, and for giving me a reassuring (and fun) support group; **Mary McClymont and Irene Lee**, for guiding me as mentors as well as funders; **Bill Ong Hing**, for providing insightful comments on the report's first draft; **Rosa Martinez, Ana Bedard, and Betty Paugh**, for helping me as "community consultants" and friends; **Vivian Vasallo and Christina Villar**, former interns, for getting this project off the ground; **Bill and Will** at **Free Hand Press**, for offering a welcome blend of professional competence and down-to-earth kindness; **Emily Goldfarb**, for giving me a real deadline; **Susan and Albert Wells** and **Windcall**, for helping me bring rocks and poetry into my life; **Mandy Gardner**, for outstanding editorial assistance and overwhelmingly kind support; **Joe and Fred,** for timely, sports-related technical assistance; **John Stover**, for researching and writing parts of this report, coordinating untold numbers of logistical details, and being the sweetest man in the world; **Laura Garcia-Melendez**, for coordinating the production of this report and standing in as my little sister; **Maurice Belanger**, for selflessly and meticulously researching the facts in the second chapter; **Frank Sharry**, for always managing to pull out a last-minute brilliant insight, and for believing in me; **David Simmons, Angela Kelley, Kathy Flewellen, Nancy Otto, Qamar Abdi, Margaret Summers, and Tracy Winston** — for editing, brainstorming, handholding, and friendship; and, finally, **Karen, Lisa, Mitzi, and Sandra**, for keeping me alive.

TABLE OF CONTENTS

"TOGETHER IN OUR DIFFERENCES"

We simply cannot enter the next century at each other's throats.... We are at a crucial crossroad in the history of this nation — and we either hang together by combating these forces that divide and degrade us or we hang separately. Do we have the intelligence, humor, imagination, courage, tolerance, love, respect, and will to meet the challenge?
— Cornel West, *Race Matters*[1]

"A CRUCIAL CROSSROAD"

Today, and throughout our nation's history, immigrants and refugees have woven themselves into the fabric of American communities. This country has evolved largely from what "newcomers" and other Americans have forged together.

Because newcomers are so immersed in our culture, Americans may have difficulty imagining a time when pizza was an exotic dish and "McDonald" a foreign name. We may even believe that America's present diversity was forged without struggle, forgetting the days when Protestant Americans lashed out against German and Irish Catholic immigrants; when, in a glaring display of both race and ethnic prejudice, the largest California newspaper declared that Chinese immigrants were "morally a far worse class to have among us than the negro"; or when a Congressional investigation concluded that immigrants from countries like Italy, Russia, and Portugal were mostly criminals, paupers, or insane people.[2]

We may also have forgotten that newcomers are not the only Americans to have been shunned as outsiders. America's history includes periods when public law forbad fourth generation Texans to speak Spanish at school, when U.S.-born Japanese Americans were thrown into detention camps, and when White industrial workers blamed high unemployment on African American migrants from the South.

America has come a long way in its progress toward justice and equality, but our accomplishments may have blinded us. Despite the challenges that each generation has faced and overcome, many Americans fail to see the connection between the experience of today's newcomers and that of their own parents and grandparents.

Legitimate concerns about jobs or education or crime have darkened our view of those who have just arrived. As we enter the second half of the 1990s, more and more Americans appear to believe that newcomers are a burden. Moreover, dramatic events in recent years — civil unrest in Los Angeles and Washington D.C., inner-city tensions between African Americans and Koreans, and a recent surge of nativist populism — have touched off a national debate about whether the increasingly diverse, multi-ethnic composition of this nation is an opportunity to embrace or a threat to resist.

John Gardner, a well-known philanthropist and advocate, has tackled these questions, arguing that

> 'Wholeness' does not characterize our cities today. They are seriously fragmented. They are torn by everything from momentary political battles to deep and complex ethnic rifts. Separate worlds live side by side but fail to communicate or understand one another... The list of substantive issues facing the city are not the city's main problem. Its main problem is that it can't pull itself to act on any of the issues. It cannot think as a community or act as a community.[3]

Gardner concludes that urban problems are not just particular issues like crime or education, but a profound lack of collective process for tackling those problems.

"Diversity" is a tough issue, but Americans cannot afford to ignore it — nor should we want to. American history proves that interaction between different race and ethnic groups generates creativity and innovation, and that scapegoating "outsiders" saps our energy and diverts our progress. The National Immigration Forum believes that newcomers are an essential part of America's future. We believe that newcomers, working side-by-side with other Americans, can help build the strong communities that are the backbone of our nation.

THE COMMUNITY INNOVATIONS PROJECT

In early 1992, the Board of Directors of the National Immigration Forum decided to take a candid look at the role of newcomers in American communities. The Board especially wanted to focus on what "race relations" does and should mean among newcomers and established residents. Up to this point the Forum, a confederation of over 200 organizations from around the country, had focused on federal immigration and refugee policy issues, such as how many immigrants the U.S. should accept, and how best to provide protection for refugees fleeing political persecution. The decision to examine human relations at the local level took the Forum in a new direction.

In 1993, the National Immigration Forum launched a new project called "Community Innovations." The goal of the Community Innovations project was to find examples of community efforts in which newcomers were working with established residents to address a shared problem.[4] Our question was not, "Where are the tensions?" but rather, "Where are the collaborations?" We hoped to learn who was working with people of different races, ethnicities, and national origins, how they were doing that work, and what all of us could do to build strong, diverse communities as well as good relations among newcomers and established residents. Community Innovations currently receives funding from the Ford Foundation, the Eugene and Agnes E. Meyer Foundation, the James Irvine Foundation, the Deer Creek Foundation, and the Charles Stewart Mott Foundation.

Community Innovations was guided by an earlier study called "Changing Relations", which conducted a six-city study of immigrant-established resident relations.[5] The Changing Relations study found that newcomers and established residents interact both frequently and well. Changing Relations documented how both groups change, and are changed by, the other. One of the project's key findings was that newcomers and established residents learn to work together because the survival of their communities depends upon it.

> When groups come together to participate in a shared task, the inspiration is usually a desire to improve specific community conditions — to secure better social services or housing, or to battle neighborhood crime and deterioration. The groups are not searching consciously for cross-cultural means to improve an abstract sense of 'quality of life.' Rather, in these situations, they are struggling together over a loss of control in the face of dramatic changes in their standard of living .... When given the opportunity, occasion, and a shared project, newcomers and established residents show a willingness to work together.[6]

Through Community Innovations, the Forum hoped to learn more about those situations in which newcomers and established residents had found the *opportunity* and *occasion* to build a *shared project*.

We launched the Community Innovations project with the belief that the best "experts" are the people actually doing the work. In the words of playwright and performance artist Anna Deveare Smith, we wanted to find "those who really speak in their own communities." Smith, whose work focuses on violent intergroup clashes such as those in New York's Crown Heights or Los Angeles' South Central, believes

Americans fail to see the connection between the experience of today's newcomers and that of their own parents and grandparents.

> There is a gap between those who are heard and those who speak .... The media most often go to experts to learn about difference. My sense is that American character lives not in one place or the other, but in the gaps between the places, and our struggle to be together in our differences.[7]

Like Smith, we set out to search for this "American character."

Of course, the scope of the Community Innovations project was limited: we looked for efforts that brought newcomers and established residents together to act on a mutual concern. Working with a committed group of local leaders, policy makers, and scholars,[8] we developed methods, definitions, and plans to help us find useful examples (See p. 11, "How Was this Project Conducted?"). We then examined a broad range of community efforts, conducting over 100 interviews with community leaders and residents of New York City, Chicago, Los Angeles, and Washington, D.C. (See p. 15, "Putting these Initiatives In Context"). We then selected 16 to present in this report, including:

■ A housing group that has taken traditional tenant organizing strategies and trans- formed them to meet the needs of an evolving mix of Latino, African, African American, and Asian residents;

■ A community credit union that has reached out and drawn in Caribbean, African, and American blacks to build a new source of economic power; and

■ A city-wide coalition advocating for high-quality adult education for African Americans and newcomers.

This report contains stories describing each initiative, conclusions we drew from them, and recommendations about what funders, policy makers, and community leaders can do to support them.

A NEW PERSPECTIVE

Community Innovations has taken just one small step toward understanding a complex set of issues. We cannot hope to exhaust the subject. However, the fact that these initiatives exist in the face of language, culture, and immigration and economic status differences is both remarkable and encouraging.

Based on the initiatives examined in this project, we conclude that:

Interaction broadens the perspective of people in both groups, allows each to learn from the expertise and skills of the other, and increases the odds of improving the quality of life for all.

1) **NEWCOMER/ESTABLISHED RESIDENT INITIATIVES CAN BE AN INSPIRING, INSTRUCTIVE, AND STRATEGIC PART OF REBUILDING AMERICAN COMMUNITIES.** The stories in this report illustrate how interaction between newcomers and established residents broadens the perspective of people in both groups, allows each to learn from the expertise and skills of the other, and increases the odds of improving the quality of life for all.

2) **HAVING A CONCRETE GOAL AND A COMMITMENT TO GOOD RELATIONS MAKES THESE INITIATIVES STRONGER AND MORE EFFECTIVE.** The initiatives we examined needed a concrete goal to motivate people to participate. But they also needed a conscientious, explicit commitment to building good relationships within their community.

3) **THESE COLLABORATIONS MADE A SERIOUS INVESTMENT IN "PROCESS."** In virtually every case we examined, the "mundane" process of talking with participants, pulling them together, and keeping them informed took the most time and had the biggest impact on what they accomplished and the relationships they built. These initiatives depend on key people who are committed to the processes that enable people to work together. These people focus not just on what an initiative wants to accomplish, but *how* it gets that done.

4) **STRONG NEWCOMER/ESTABLISHED RESIDENT INITIATIVES COMPLEMENT, RATHER THAN REPLACE, ORGANIZATIONS THAT REPRESENT THE PEOPLE OF ONE RACE, ETHNIC, OR NATIONAL ORIGIN.** Many of the most promising initiatives we studied saw themselves as complementing, rather than replacing, existing single-group organizations.

These conclusions are described in more detail, accompanied by specific recommendations for ways to improve the quality of life in diverse American communities, later in the report.

A NEW OPPORTUNITY

The National Immigration Forum believes that the Community Innovations findings can guide funders, policy makers, and community leaders who want to rebuild American communities. As our recommendations describe, the types of grants made by funders, and who they are made to can have a dramatic impact on the communities where newcomers and established residents live. Policy makers can also play an important role in raising the awareness and understanding of diverse communities, and in seeking ways to incorporate positive intergroup interaction into other program and policy goals. Finally, community organizations, in partnership with funders and policy makers, can use these findings to launch their own innovative practices and projects.

This project has also helped the Forum clarify its own perspective by reinvigorating our commitment to efforts that recognize newcomers as leaders who serve the broad interests of their communities. This project also gave us a deeper understanding of the challenges that immigration can pose for established residents and the need to reflect on our own assumptions and practices. New issues and organizations were brought to our attention, and we became aware of many potential new allies. As a result, we are exploring new ways that we and our members can collaborate with groups outside the traditional immigrant/refugee networks.

A TIME FOR CAUTIOUS OPTIMISM

The National Immigration Forum believes that the future of America's communities depends on how newcomers and established residents learn to work together. Coming together in our differences won't be easy, but we remain cautiously optimistic. A recent survey found that Americans would be willing to set aside their most negative views and work with people from another group *to solve some of the most pressing problems of their neighborhoods and communities.*[9] In the words of Henry Cisneros, Secretary of Housing and Urban Development and former Mayor of San Antonio, Texas:

> The decisive questions in America's civic and democratic future are those concerning whether it will be truly possible to incorporate ideas of multi-cultural inclusiveness into our institutions and our decision-making structures… We are a multi-cultural, multi-racial society and we will continuously become more so. The real question is whether we can once again create a uniquely American future. The challenge is to anticipate the changes and forge a social contract that is imaginative, and inclusive, and that rewrites the rules of human history in an American way once again.[10]

This report demonstrates that however small and unique newcomer/established resident initiatives may be, they do exist. These flickering sparks offer glimpses of bright possibility, and a future without threat of "the fire next time." [11]

How Was This Project Conducted?

What did the Forum want to learn?

The National Immigration Forum undertook this project to learn how to build community-based efforts in which newcomers and established residents worked together for the benefit of all. We approached the project with a commitment to finding information and making recommendations that could be put to practical use. Our goal was to take our experience as a coalition and use it to identify and analyze some good examples of newcomer/established resident collaboration, and stimulate action based on them. The definitions and methods we used reflect subjective decisions about what we could best accomplish and how we could be most useful.

Who designed the project?

Project Director Julie Quiroz worked with the Community Innovation's Advisory Committee to develop the project's definitions, scope, and work plan. The Advisory Committee, which included community leaders, government officials, and scholars, provided on-going feedback and guidance and also participated in two meetings held in Washington, D.C.

When was the project conducted?

The project was conducted over the eighteen-month period between January 1993 and June 1994.

What was the project looking for?

Community Innovations set out to find "promising community initiatives in which newcomers and established residents of diverse races and ethnicities work to solve common problems."

What do the terms "newcomer" and "established resident" mean?

"Newcomer" is a loosely defined term referring to recent immigrants and refugees. "Recent" can mean different things in different communities. We use the term to refer to the most recent wave of immigrants and refugees in a particular community, generally those who arrived after 1965.

"Established resident" refers to people who were born in the United States, and/or have lived here a long time. Like "newcomer," "established resident" is a fairly subjective term, but one that helps calls attention to subtle distinctions, such as the differences between recently-arrived and established members of the same national origin group. We adopted the terms "newcomer" and "established resident" from the 1993 Changing Relations project.

How does the project define "promising community initiative"?

We created two definitions, one for "promising" and one for "community initiative." Something was an "initiative" if it involved both established residents and newcomers, was locally based, sought to solve a problem, consisted of individuals and/or organizations voluntarily participating in an on-going set of activities, and had an organizational structure. We considered an initiative "promising" if participants, using their own definition, reported that it was "promising," both newcomers and established residents were making a substantive and active contribution to defining and addressing the problem, the effort resulted in some concrete change, and the effort offered some lessons for other communities.

What did the project exclude?

This project did not examine efforts that were taking place at the national level, those that focused exclusively on changing individual attitudes (without changing the individual's situation), or those that people participated in as part of a job or class requirement. We also excluded efforts which did not follow a goal of establishing a continuous process or permanent structure. Examples of things we did not examine include: national summits and conferences, prejudice reduction seminars, multicultural dialogues focused exclusively on intergroup relations, casual interactions (e.g., on the street, in stores, etc.), work place diversity training, and multicultural curricula for schools.

Our decision to exclude these efforts reflected our experience working with intergroup coalitions, our judgment (given our expertise) about what types of efforts we could best access, analyze, and put to practical use, and our desire to examine the many community roles that immigrants play, roles that the media and others often fail to explore.

Why didn't this project analyze "failures"?

While we understood the value of analyzing "failures," we wanted this project to offer a counterweight to the negative views of diversity often portrayed in the media.

WHAT GEOGRAPHIC AREAS WERE STUDIED AND WHY?

Community Innovations examined initiatives in metropolitan Chicago, Los Angeles, New York and Washington, D.C. We chose these areas because they have growing newcomer populations, are geographically distinct, and have received national and local media attention for problems related to race and ethnic differences. We were also familiar with many individuals and networks active in these cities.

HOW WERE THE INITIATIVES IDENTIFIED?

Advisory Community members and other local leaders helped us identify a preliminary list of people to contact and initiatives to visit. The Project Director, aided by local "community consultants," then conducted individual interviews with leaders and participants and observed different community activities, such as meetings and events.

HOW WERE THE INITIATIVES IN THIS BOOK SELECTED?

We selected efforts which most nearly fit the project's definition of a promising initiative and which were particularly interesting, innovative, or illustrative of key issues. This report includes detailed stories about some initiatives and brief "snapshots" of others.

WHAT ABOUT INITIATIVES THE PROJECT DIDN'T FIND?

There are undoubtedly many initiatives we did not uncover. As our goal was to find, examine, and describe interesting examples, we do not claim that the initiatives we have included are typical of what is going on in communities, that they are the only models, or that they represent the range of possible approaches.

HOW DID THE PROJECT GET FEEDBACK FROM PEOPLE IN THE INITIATIVES?

The Project Director conducted individual conversations with representatives from each of the initiatives and asked for their comments on drafts of this report. In addition, we held group meetings in Washington D.C., Chicago, and Los Angeles to discuss the findings and direction of the project.

PUTTING THESE INITIATIVES IN CONTEXT

Without some redistribution of wealth and power, downward mobility and debilitating poverty will continue to drive people into desperate channels. And without principled opposition to xenophobias from above and below, these desperate channels will produce a cold-hearted and mean-spirited America no longer worth fighting for or living in.

—Cornel West, *Race Matters*

The question of how newcomers fit into American communities — especially urban communities — has never been more important than right now. During the 1980s, more than seven million immigrants came to the United States, the largest number since the first decade of this century. For every one hundred Americans, nine are newcomers and another ten have a parent who is a newcomer. The vast majority of newcomers (93 percent) live in urban areas like Miami, Los Angeles, and New York, in which newcomers make up more than a quarter of all residents.[12]

More and more newcomers are people of color. In the 1950s, U.S. immigration quotas ensured that two-thirds of all newcomers came from Europe and Canada.[13] Then, in 1965, the growing civil rights movement contributed to the passage of national legislation which eliminated these discriminatory quotas. Since the quotas were abolished, the proportion of immigrants from Asia, Latin America, and the Caribbean has grown dramatically.

Today's newcomers enter American urban areas at a challenging time. Many cities, including those discussed in this report, face dwindling tax revenues and growing poverty, as well as seemingly intractable problems like crime and homelessness. Urban areas across the nation are still picking up the pieces where once-thriving factories have shut down or relocated, leaving residents to scramble for fewer jobs at lower wages. And the gap between rich and poor — which often separates whites from people of color — has grown to shocking size.

Newcomers often start out alongside low-income neighbors.[14] While disadvantaged groups such as African Americans continue to struggle with continued economic, political and social marginalization, immigration is adding more than a million people to the U.S. population each year. Years of reliable research have found that immigration generally has a tiny negative impact on low-income African Americans and, in some cases, actually has a beneficial impact.[15] Nonetheless, the perceived economic competition remains an emotional and divisive issue among newcomers and established residents.

WHO LIVES IN THESE CITIES?

	NEW YORK CITY (METRO*)	CHICAGO CITY (METRO)	LOS ANGELES CITY (METRO)	WASHINGTON CITY (METRO)
AFRICAN AMERICAN	29% (18%)	39% (19%)	14% (9%)	66% (27%)
ASIAN	7% (5%)	4% (3%)	10% (9%)	2% (5%)
LATINO**	24% (15%)	20% (11%)	40% (33%)	5% (6%)
WHITE	52% (70%)	45% (72%)	53% (65%)	30% (66%)

▶ WHITES ARE THE LARGEST RACIAL GROUP IN THE CITIES OF NEW YORK, CHICAGO, AND LOS ANGELES; AFRICAN AMERICANS ARE THE LARGEST RACIAL GROUP IN THE CITY OF WASHINGTON, DC.

▶ TWO IN FIVE LOS ANGELES CITY RESIDENTS ARE LATINO.

▶ IN WASHINGTON, DC, ASIANS AND LATINOS ARE MORE LIKELY TO LIVE IN THE SUBURBS THAN IN THE CITY. THIS IS NOT TRUE IN ANY OF THE OTHER METROPOLITAN AREAS.

Source: 1990 Census

*For New York, Chicago, and Los Angeles, "Metro" refers to the Consolidated Metropolitan Statistical Area (CMSA) which includes the city and other nearby urban areas. The Washington Metropolitan Statistical Area (MSA) includes Washington and surrounding suburban towns and counties.

**The Census includes Latinos under both African American and White, therefore percentages may add up to more than 100.

HOW DID THE POPULATION IN THESE AREAS CHANGE IN THE 1980S?

	NEW YORK CITY (METRO*)	CHICAGO CITY (METRO)	LOS ANGELES CITY (METRO)	WASHINGTON CITY (METRO)
AFRICAN AMERICAN	+18% (+16%)	-9% (-1%)	-4% (+16%)	-11% (+20%)
ASIAN	+122% (+135%)	+51% (+77%)	+74% (+138%)	+69% (+144%)
LATINO**	+27% (+35%)	+29% (+41%)	+70% (+73%)	+85% (+137%)
WHITE	-11% (+6%)	-15% (-1%)	+2% (+11%)	+5% (+24%)
TOTAL POPULATION	+4% (+3%)	-7% (+2%)	+16% (+26%)	-5% (+5%)

▶ ASIANS WERE THE FASTEST GROWING POPULATION IN THE CITIES AND METROPOLITAN AREAS OF NEW YORK, CHICAGO, AND LOS ANGELES. IN THE CITY OF WASHINGTON, THE LATINO POPULATION GREW THE FASTEST, WHILE THE ASIAN POPULATION GREW FASTEST IN THE METROPOLITAN AREA OVERALL.

▶ THE AFRICAN-AMERICAN POPULATION DECLINED IN THE CITIES OF CHICAGO, LOS ANGELES, AND WASHINGTON. HOWEVER, IN THE METROPOLITAN AREAS OF LOS ANGELES AND WASHINGTON, THE AFRICAN-AMERICAN POPULATION GREW.

Source: 1980 and 1990 Census

*For New York, Chicago, and Los Angeles, "Metro" refers to the Consolidated Metropolitan Statistical Area (CMSA) which includes the city and other nearby urban areas. The Washington Metropolitan Statistical Area (MSA) includes Washington and surrounding suburban towns and counties.

**The Census includes Latinos under both African American and White, therefore percentages may add up to more than 100.

WHAT'S THE NEWCOMER POPULATION LIKE IN THESE AREAS?

	NEW YORK	CHICAGO	LOS ANGELES	WASHINGTON
FOREIGN BORN AMONG CITY RESIDENTS (1990)	28%	17%	38%	10%
GROWTH IN CITY'S FOREIGN-BORN POPULATION 1980-1990	84%	79%	130%	136%
CITY'S FOREIGN-BORN WHO ARE NATURALIZED CITIZENS* (1990)	42%	38%	25%	29%
TOP FOREIGN BORN GROUPS AMONG CITY RESIDENTS (BY COUNTRY, 1990)	DOMINICAN REPUBLIC JAMAICA CHINA ITALY SOVIET UNION	MEXICO POLAND PHILIPPINES KOREA GERMANY	MEXICO EL SALVADOR GUATEMALA PHILIPPINES KOREA	EL SALVADOR JAMAICA UNITED KINGDOM PHILIPPINES ETHIOPIA

▶ NEARLY TWO FIFTHS OF LOS ANGELES CITY RESIDENTS, AND MORE THAN ONE QUARTER OF NEW YORK CITY RESIDENTS WERE BORN OUTSIDE THE U.S.

▶ DURING THE 1980S, THE FOREIGN-BORN POPULATION OF EACH CITY GREW FASTER THAN THE NATIVE BORN POPULATION.

▶ THE FOREIGN-BORN POPULATION GREW FASTEST IN WASHINGTON AND LOS ANGELES.

Source: 1990 Census
*"Citizens" refers to those who have passed all citizenship requirements. Does not include legal permanent residents and other legal immigrants.

WHAT ARE THE FUTURE TRENDS IN IMMIGRATION TO THESE AREAS?

	NEW YORK	CHICAGO	LOS ANGELES	WASHINGTON
U.S. IMMIGRANTS WHO PLAN TO SETTLE IN METRO AREA (1992)	13%	4%	13%	3%
TOP NEW IMMIGRANT GROUPS WHO PLAN TO SETTLE IN METRO AREA (BY COUNTRY, 1992)	DOMINICAN REPUBLIC SOVIET UNION CHINA	POLAND MEXICO INDIA	MEXICO EL SALVADOR PHILIPPINES	VIETNAM EL SALVADOR INDIA

▶ METROPOLITAN WASHINGTON IS LIKELY TO SEE AN INCREASE IN ITS VIETNAMESE POPULATION.

▶ AMONG NEWCOMERS ARRIVING IN THE CHICAGO METROPOLITAN AREA, POLES MAY OUTNUMBER MEXICANS IN THE COMING YEARS.

▶ METROPOLITAN NEW YORK AND LOS ANGELES WILL CONTINUE TO RECEIVE THE LARGEST PROPORTION OF NEWCOMERS IN THE COUNTRY.

Source: Statistical Yearbook of the Immigration and Naturalization Service, 1992.

NEW YORK: UNENDING VARIATION

New York is the most diverse city in America. For decades, the five boroughs have been the destination of choice for immigrants from around the world. An unending variation of human endeavor is found in our city, and that diversity is our greatest strength. Our diversity contributes to our economic and cultural vitality, and makes us home to the innovative and the unique. In New York, diversity has been a boon, not a burden.

—Rudolf W. Guiliani, Mayor of New York[16]

AMERICA'S "GATEWAY CITY." For many Americans, New York defines the term "gateway city." New York City receives more immigrants than any other city in the country. In the mid-nineteenth century, roughly one in five New Yorkers came from Ireland. By 1930, New York was home to nearly 40 percent of this country's Russian immigrants and a quarter of all Italian immigrants.[17]

NEGOTIATING DIVERSITY. New York houses some of the most diverse communities in the world, including Elmhurst, Queens, with its 17,000 recent immigrants from 112 different countries.[18] While different race and ethnic groups tend to cluster together — Dominicans in Washington Heights, Caribbeans in Central Brooklyn, whites in Manhattan — New Yorkers negotiate race and ethnic differences every day.

NEGATIVE IMMIGRANT IMAGES. In 1993, New York was the site of two dramatic incidents that shaped national immigration policy debate. In that year, the bombing of the World Trade Center by Islamic fundamentalists generated widespread concern about terrorists' ability to enter the U.S. through legal means. Later that year, the Long Island Railroad commuter murders allegedly committed by a Jamaican man caught national attention and reinforced growing anti-immigrant sentiment.

FLASHPOINTS OF CONFLICT. In recent years, New York's Brooklyn borough has received widespread media attention for dramatic examples of intergroup violence. In May 1990 the Church Avenue boycott began when black Caribbeans accused a Korean store employee of attacking a Haitian woman. For four months, outraged blacks picketed the store and discouraged shoppers from patronizing it. While some blacks, including a contingent of students from nearby Erasmus Hall high school, rejected the boycott, it nonetheless came to symbolize African American resentment of Asian merchants who appear to thrive in otherwise struggling neighborhoods.

In Crown Heights, Brooklyn, African American and Caribbean black residents have long believed that Lubavitchers — an orthodox Jewish sect that fled from Nazi Germany

— mistreat area blacks and receive preferential treatment from the city. In August 1991, tensions between the two groups exploded when a car carrying the Lubavitcher leader crashed into and killed a seven-year-old boy from Guyana, and seriously injured his cousin. Angered by rumors that a Lubavitch-run ambulance had ignored the injured children, blacks in the area turned on the police and the Lubavitchers, who in turn responded with force and violence. The night of the crash, a second tragedy occurred when a group of young black men stabbed to death a 29-year-old Lubavitcher. The violence between blacks, Lubavitchers, and police lasted for three days.

Los Angeles: Urban Galaxy

Who has anticipated, or adjusted to, the scale of change in Southern California over the last fifteen years? … [W]ith a built-up surface area nearly the size of Ireland and a GNP bigger than India's — the urban galaxy dominated by Los Angeles is the fastest growing metropolis in the advanced industrial world.
—Mike Davis, *City of Quartz*[19]

VASTNESS AND MOTION. Los Angeles is huge. The city covers 465 square miles, and the metropolitan area more than 2,186 square miles.[9] It is a city of motion, where most people get around by freeway and one-seventh of the population has lived there less than ten years.[20]

GEOGRAPHIC LINES. On Los Angeles' West Side, the vast majority of residents are white. Drive a half an hour, however, and you find what demographers have dubbed a Latino "mega-barrio" — a 193 square-mile area including East Los Angeles, Pico Union, and parts of downtown. Three-fourths of this area's population is Latino, with Mexicans dominating in East Los Angeles and Central Americans dominating in Pico Union. Asian and Pacific Islanders congregate in ethnic enclaves such as Little Tokyo and Koreatown, but are most heavily concentrated outside the city of Los Angeles, in adjacent metropolitan areas such as Monterey Park. South Central Los Angeles, once home to the majority of Los Angeles' African American population, has experienced a large outflow of African Americans moving into municipalities on South Central's west and south borders.[21]

GROWING ANTI-IMMIGRANT SENTIMENT. In recent years public opinion among Californians has become more and more hostile toward immigration. This growing anti-immigrant sentiment parallels the state's recent fiscal crisis. After years of economic boom, fueled by immigrant labor, California is now suffering the impact of a recent recession and decades of disinvestment in public services.[22] In November 1994 Californians passed a statewide ballot initiative called "Proposition 187." Proposition 187 was designed to cut off undocumented immigrants from public benefits and services, and bar undocumented children from public schools. Although law suits currently prevent the new law from taking effect, its passage has already resulted in hardship and discrimination among California residents who appear "foreign."

NEW PLAYERS IN THE RACE DRAMA. When it comes to the issues of race and ethnic relations, Los Angeles has burned a lasting image on the minds of people around the globe. The 1992 acquittal of four police officers in the Rodney King beating, and the ensuing three days of violence and destruction, shook the nation and the world. Moreover, this "uprising" illustrated the complexity of today's race and ethnic relations. According to playwright and performance artist Anna Deveare Smith, "Whereas Jewish merchants were hit during the [1965] Watts riots, Korean merchants were hit this time. Although the media tended to focus on blacks in South-Central, the Latino population was equally involved. We tend to think of race as us and them — us or them being black or white depending on one's own color. The relationships among peoples of color and within racial groups are getting more and more complicated."

CHICAGO: COLORFUL SPRAWL

[Chicago's] neighborhoods originated most often as gleams in the eyes of ambitious land developers or as ethnic enclaves, which grew into towns that were in turn swallowed up by the swelling, 19th-century city. The result was and continues to be a diverse and colorful sprawl of traditional and newly hybrid communities and cultures. Less benign influences in these enclaves include both subtle and overt expressions of nationalism, xenophobia, and outright racism for which, unfortunately, Chicago is also known.[23]
—*Sweet Home Chicago*

A PORT OF ENTRY. Americans do not tend to think of Chicago as a major "port of entry." But themes of migration and change dominate the city's history. Chicago was founded in the eighteenth century by a Spanish-speaking black Caribbean. In the nineteenth century, Chicago boasted the third largest concentration of Germans in the world. Chicago's turn-of-the-century immigrant settlement houses became internationally-recognized models of community-based services and activism. And it is in Chicago that

African American migrants from the South first plugged a Delta rhythm into an urban electric current, producing the high-energy sound known as the "Chicago Blues."[24] Today, Chicago is home to millions of newcomers and remains a city of ongoing transformation.

CITY OF NEIGHBORHOODS. Chicago has been called "a vast mosaic of separate entities, each with its own history, personality, and particular landmarks and institutions."[25] With names like "Greektown" and "Ukranian Village," immigration's legacy lingers on in Chicago's neighborhoods. At the same time, recent newcomers are transforming the areas where they settle. For example, "Back of the Yards," made famous in Upton Sinclair's *The Jungle* and Saul Alinsky's pioneering community organizing efforts in the 1930s, has shed its East European and Irish past to assume its present Latino incarnation. Uptown, which was settled by Swedes early in this century, is now dominated by a mix of Latino and Asian groups.

> *It is in Chicago that African American migrants from the South first plugged a Delta rhythm into an urban electric current, producing the high-energy sound known as the "Chicago Blues."*

PERIODIC CONFLICT. Although Chicago has not experienced the well-publicized race and ethnic conflicts of other American cities, the Chicago Bulls' victories in the 1991 and 1992 National Basketball Association Championships resulted in looting and violence. Korean store owners in African American communities were among the groups most seriously victimized during the disturbances.

MULTI-ETHNIC POLITICS. For a brief period in the early 1980s, Chicago became a symbol of multi-racial, multi-ethnic political reform. In 1983, a diverse block of African American, white, and Latino voters elected Harold Washington as Chicago's first African American mayor. During his four-year tenure, Washington's "rainbow coalition" sought unprecedented reform and inclusiveness. When Washington died suddenly of a heart attack in 1987, a "caretaker" mayor took the reins and the coalition quickly fell apart. In 1989, Chicago politics came full circle with the election of Richard M. Daley, son of "Boss" Richard J. — Chicago's iron-fisted mayor of the period 1955 to 1976.

WASHINGTON, D.C.: SOCIO-CULTURAL CHASMS

The District of Columbia contains one of the greatest concentrations of affluent, college-educated blacks in the country. The percentage of blacks who live in upscale neighborhoods is triple the U.S. average, far ahead, even, of Atlanta. But suburban flight has steadily depleted the number of affluent D.C. blacks. In fact, most of the area's African Americans now live in the suburbs. Taking their place in the city have been many Latinos and many ... highly educated, monied whites who are the quiet force behind the District's sociocultural chasms.
—*The Washington Post* [26]

CAPITAL STATUS. Historically, most migrants to the nation's capital were southern African Americans who sought the relatively high-wage jobs found in government and government-related business. Today, two in three Washington, D.C. residents is African American and one in five residents works for the federal government. Because Washington is a federal district, not a state, its Congresspeople do not have the full voting authority of other Congressional delegations. At the same time, Congress wields enormous power in a broad range of district policies, including its budget.

NEWCOMERS: FEW BUT GROWING. In a reversal of a seventy-year decline, the proportion of Washington, D.C. residents born outside the United States grew from five percent in 1970 to seven percent in 1980.[27] Many of these recent newcomers are Central Americans who came to Washington to escape civil war and political upheaval in El Salvador and Guatemala. In an equally important trend, the newcomer population of areas like Arlington, Virginia, directly across the river from Washington, has skyrocketed. According to the 1990 Census one-fifth of Arlington residents were born outside the United States. In 1990 two percent of Washington residents were Asian or Pacific Islander, compared with seven percent in the suburban county of Arlington (VA) and more than eight percent in Fairfax County (VA) and Montgomery County (MD). Latinos made up only five percent of the District's 1990 population, compared with 13 percent in Arlington County, seven percent in Montgomery County, and six percent in Fairfax County.[28]

SPARKS OF FRUSTRATION. On May 5, 1991, the police shooting of Salvadoran newcomer Daniel Enrique Gomez sparked what came to be known as the "Mount Pleasant Riots" — three days of unrest in which 175 people were arrested for rioting and violating an emergency curfew. Although the police worked with the controversial help of the

Immigration and Naturalization Service (INS) to target undocumented Latino rioters, police records indicate that less than half of the people actually arrested during the three-day period were Latinos.[29] Public reaction nevertheless focused, often negatively, on Latinos. For example, Latino activists became outraged when news reports quoted some African American leaders' belief that the looters were immigrants who should be deported.

Latino activists went on to organize the Latino Civil Rights Task Force, which argued that city policies and practices, such as police harassment of Latinos and discrimination against Latinos in city government employment, had contributed to the frustration behind the unrest.[30] In 1993 a U.S. Commission on Civil Rights investigation report validated all the Task Force charges.[31]

COMMUNITY INNOVATIONS:

HOUSING

FOR TENANTS, COLLABORATION STARTS AT HOME

WASHINGTON, DC— *The resident association leaders hold their meeting in the laundry room of their apartment building. The atmosphere is relaxed and intimate; after years together as a tenant organization and now as cooperative owners, these are people who know each other well. Habib, an Ethiopian with eight years in the building, proposes that association leaders from each nationality — Americans of African descent, Salvadorans, Ethiopians, other Africans — talk with residents from their own group to help with upkeep of the building. Catherine, an African American who has lived in the building for 20 years, supports Habib's approach and beams with pride when discussing the resident association. "When people have been working together a long time you're like family," she says. "We want to be together more than apart." Habib agrees: "The tenants' association is when the first interaction [among residents] started. The barrier was broken."*

IN THE LAUNDRY ROOM

CHANGING WITH THE TIMES

Habib and Catherine's resident association came to life with the support of Washington Inner City Self-Help (WISH), a sixteen-year-old community organizing project which operates from a church basement. A coalition of churches led by African American clergy founded WISH to help tenants fight the rent hikes and evictions that start when landlords want to attract higher income residents. WISH has continued this work over the years but, like many housing groups across the country, has expanded its focus to include "cooperative development" through which tenants organize and actually purchase their buildings.

Over the years, WISH has struggled to reach out to a tenant population that grows more and more diverse each day. In the 1980s, thousands of Central American newcomers settled in northwest Washington neighborhoods like Mount Pleasant and Columbia Heights, where African Americans predominated and WISH had long been active. In ten years, the Latino population in these areas grew by 131 percent. Paul Battle, WISH's African American director, says that nowadays "in this part of Washington, it's hard to go to a building and not find a mixture of folks living there."

But WISH believes that exploitation, not diversity, is the community's problem. According to Battle, who has been organizing communities for twenty years, landlords and developers are using newfound differences in race, ethnicity, and immigration status to weaken residents' collective power. Battle argues that landlords are utilizing a new version of the "block busting" long directed at African American communities. "Land-lords will bring in Latinos and encourage a situation where blacks get mad at the overcrowding or noise," says Battle. "They want to run blacks out because they tend to be under rent control; they can get Latinos to pay more. The solution is to educate and organize both groups."

COMMITMENT TO THE BASICS

WISH's unique perspective — and decades of commitment to basic community organizing — has laid a foundation on which tenants of different races and ethnicities can work together. WISH still follows the community organizing principles pioneered in the 1930s by Chicago activist Saul Alinsky. For example, WISH believes that community leaders, rather than staff, should set agendas and carry them out, that the media can be an important tool, and that confrontation is sometimes the only option for getting something done. WISH starts with the basics: meeting with public housing tenants whose walls are cracked and ceilings are falling down or commercial housing tenants whose rents will skyrocket if their landlord sells their building to a profit-hungry developer. WISH tries to nurture leaders among the tenants and help them develop a strategy to achieve their objectives. Sometimes a strategy can mean picketing, sometimes lawsuits. WISH offers technical advice, and training to resident groups, and works with financial and government institutions to secure loans that are normally out of the reach of low-income neighborhoods.

NAME:	WASHINGTON INNER CITY SELF-HELP (WISH)
PARTICIPANTS:	AFRICAN AMERICANS, CENTRAL AMERICAN, AFRICAN, AND ASIAN NEWCOMERS
GOAL:	DECENT, AFFORDABLE HOUSING IN A DIVERSE COMMUNITY
OBSERVATIONS:	COMMUNITY ORGANIZING ACROSS RACIAL/ETHNIC LINES HELPS PREVENT EXPLOITATION OF DIFFERENCES AND PROMOTES ACTION ON URGENT COMMUNITY NEEDS
INNOVATION:	HELPING DIVERSE TENANTS UNITE FOR COMMUNITY IMPROVEMENT

STEPS TOWARD CHANGE

Organizing among diverse tenants presents some very real challenges, even for an organization with WISH's experience. WISH's first step was to hire staff that reflect the area's diversity. For many years, WISH's staff was entirely African American. Today, the staff includes one African American and one Latino organizer, as well as a part-time organizer (and co-op association member) from Ethiopia. WISH has also made the most of a tight budget by trying innovative "temporary" solutions. For example, WISH has worked with volunteer interpreters from the Chinatown Cultural Center in tenant meetings that include Chinese residents.

WISH has also struggled to ensure that representatives of each race and ethnic group help shape the overall direction. The organization has attempted to promote leadership among newcomer groups by identifying and mentoring emerging leaders, conducting board meetings in each language ("We timed it," says Battle, "it really only adds about 15 minutes.") and avoiding isolation by making sure there is more than one representative of a particular race or ethnic group in a meeting. WISH has also established a Latino Caucus and convened meetings with African community leaders to discuss the needs and priorities of specific populations.

Even when Latinos are not present at a meeting, WISH encourages its African American members to think about how to keep Latinos involved. At a meeting to discuss an upcoming community congress, African American tenant leaders talked about ways to accommodate the schedules of Latinos, who tend to hold second jobs and have a hard time participating in evening events. WISH now has Latino representation on its board and is recognized in the Latino community, but the challenge remains. Many housing residents are Latino and African newcomers, but few hold leadership positions in resident associations that would ensure them a seat on WISH's board.

> *"They want to run blacks out because they tend to be under rent control; they can get Latinos to pay more. The solution is to educate and organize both groups."*

WISH tries to improve the attitudes and perceptions different groups have about each other. WISH housing organizer Benito Diaz believes that keeping different groups together is "difficult but workable. African Americans complain about Salvadorans' lack of cleanliness and Salvadorans complain about African American crime. We try to get them to fight the landlord, not each other." Still, WISH staff concede that more could be done to change attitudes even while focusing on a common goal. For example, a few years ago WISH held an all-day meeting to discuss differences and commonalities between groups. Like many community organizations, however, such efforts remain a luxury for WISH. "There's a role for sharing experience," says Paul Battle, "but we need money for basic stuff we're doing. [Race and ethnic] issues should be addressed and need to be addressed, but how much time is there for it?" WISH struggles to find financial support for its work, and currently relies on funding from churches, local foundations, banks, and the United Way.

MAKING A DIFFERENCE

WISH's commitment to diversity has helped it continue to make an impact on the community. Recently, WISH worked with a group of Latino and African American tenants whose landlord saw potential profits if he could get rid of the tenants and sell the building. The landlord tried to force the tenants out by cutting off the heat and refusing to cooperate with efforts to drive out nearby drug dealers. With WISH's help, the tenants pressured the landlord to sell them the building, then obtained funds to improve that building through "linkage dollars" — money contributed by private developers to satisfy the city's requirement that they build housing. This financial arrangement was a major victory for the building residents and a precedent-setting strategy for tenants throughout the city.

Conclusion

WISH is still working to perfect a model of intergroup organizing — and to ensure that WISH itself survives as a solid, financially stable community institution. Some, like Benito Diaz, believe WISH must find a way to address a "very real element of racism" that makes it hard for groups to work together. But the organizing goes on. In the view of Muhammad, a co-op association leader from Sierre Leone, "We are here with a goal. When you're fighting to reach a goal, you don't have time to go fighting needlessly. We don't have time to be hating ourselves."

REFUGEE GROUPS BUILD AFFORDABLE HOUSING AND NEW RELATIONSHIPS

CHICAGO, IL— *For Eric Butler, the chance to buy a town home was a dream come true. "After being cramped in an apartment and [enduring] a lot of rough times, to come into a home is fantastic," Butler gushes. Butler,*

A DREAM COME TRUE

who is African American and grew up in Chicago, now lives in a new housing development called "International Homes."

Eric tells the story about meeting his new International Homes neighbor, Santiago, who struggled to speak English. Eric quickly fetched his daughters who attend a bilingual elementary school nearby, and introduced them to Santiago. When they began speaking Spanish, Santiago was overcome with emotion. "It meant so much to have an American child speak Spanish to him," says Butler. "It was good for us and for him to know that his culture is important to us."

DEFINING THE NEEDS OF A DIVERSE COMMUNITY

Eric and Santiago didn't become neighbors by accident. "International Homes," a development of 28 affordable town homes, came into existence because local refugee leaders in Chicago's Uptown area decided it was time to bring affordable home ownership to their area. These refugee leaders did not work in isolation but joined with a long-established community organization to ensure that community members of different race and ethnic backgrounds participated in the project's development and benefited from its completion.

Uptown for decades served as an immigrant port-of-entry, welcoming newcomer residents from countries like Vietnam, Africa, Mexico, and Romania. These newcomers live alongside established residents which include Native Americans, African Americans, and whites from Appalachia, making Uptown Chicago's most diverse community.

Less than one-fifth of Uptown's residents own their own home. Residents who *move up* economically usually *move out* to buy a home. Unfortunately, these outmigrants often take their community ties and economic power with them when they go. "The community itself was changing," observes Dr. Erku Yimir, Executive Director of the Ethiopian Community Association in Uptown. "It was becoming more established, having more than survival needs, relating more with other groups." Yimir's organization is one of Uptown's many mutual assistance associations ("MAAs"), refugee-run organizations created to provide community-based services to newly arrived refugees. In communities around the country, MAAs have served as the life-blood to recent arrivals trying to survive in dizzyingly new and complicated surroundings. Now, as earlier newcomers have become more established and refugee program funding less secure, many MAAs are struggling to redefine their roles.

REACHING OUT BEYOND REFUGEE COMMUNITIES

In 1991, Uptown's MAAs — including the Cambodian Association of Illinois, the Chinese Mutual Aid Association, the Vietnamese Association of Illinois, the Ethiopian Community Association of Chicago, and the Lao American Community Services — launched the International Homes project with Voice of the People, a local community development organization. For years the MAAs had met each month to discuss rental housing issues. It was here that the MAAs began to discuss the problem of outmigration. The MAAs agreed that Uptown needed its established immigrants to keep the area's economic base strong and to preserve its ethnic diversity.

NAME:	INTERNATIONAL HOMES
PARTICIPANTS:	ASIAN AND AFRICAN REFUGEES, NATIVE AMERICANS, AFRICAN AMERICANS
GOAL:	AFFORDABLE HOME OWNERSHIP IN A DIVERSE COMMUNITY
OBSERVATIONS:	AS IMMIGRANT COMMUNITIES GET MORE ESTABLISHED, THEIR NEEDS CHANGE AND THE POTENTIAL FOR COLLABORATION GROWS
INNOVATION:	HOME OWNERSHIP THAT STRENGTHENS DIVERSE COMMUNITIES; COMMITMENT TO REAL PARTICIPATION OF MANY GROUPS IN DESIGN, IMPLEMENTATION

This collaboration was new for both the MAAs and Voice. For Janet Hasz, Voice's Executive Director, International Homes presented an opportunity to build housing and new relationships. According to Hasz, "This project really helps immigrants *and* low-income communities. Neither of these groups has the paper trail of finances that banks usually require to get mortgage loans." One of Voice's first steps was to establish an International Homes steering committee that included both the MAAs and non-refugee organizations, such as the American Indian Economic Development Association.

PURSUING A DUAL GOAL

The steering committee's goal was to build affordable town homes and make them available to a diverse group of Uptown residents. International Homes would hold a lottery for residents meeting certain basic requirements. The winners would get a chance to buy a town home, and Voice's ongoing support and guidance to help them get through the paperwork and financing that intimidates so many first-time home buyers.

The *process* of bringing different groups together was also important. Voice understood this and invested time and energy sorting through mundane but critical questions like how frequently to meet and how much information everyone needed before a meeting. "Mutual aid societies were active participants, not tokens," says Erku Yimir of the Ethiopian Community Association. "Anything that required a decision of the group required a meeting. The Voice of the People made sure that everyone had the information they needed to participate. The steering committee was effective because there was open information sharing, good pre-meeting discussion and agenda-setting, and decisions were made at a slower pace."

MAKING HOMEOWNERSHIP POSSIBLE

Shrewd financial know-how was also key. International Homes secured funds from a national nonprofit housing organization, the Local Initiatives Support Corporation (LISC), to

> *"They will be an interesting new voice in the community," predicts Hasz. "Home owners had always been the rich people."*

support the project's start-up phase. They took advantage of a city program called New Homes for Chicago, which provided $20,000 in subsidies for vacant lots. International Homes also got assistance and loans from private banks under the Community Reinvestment Act (CRA), legislation that requires banks to return some of their profit back into economically depressed areas. They then worked with the banks through the Federal Home Loan Bank's Affordable Housing Program to secure down payment assistance, closing cost subsidies, and low interest rates for prospective buyers. The steering committee also convinced a private bank to fund the printing and distribution of home buyer training materials translated into five languages.

THE DREAM BECOMES REALITY

Three years after the steering committee began, International Homes is a reality. Twenty-eight families moved into their new homes in the Spring of 1994. These families include African American and Native American established residents and newcomers from eleven different countries, including Vietnam, Ethiopia, Nigeria, and Mexico. Residents like Eric and Santiago are also learning to work together. International Homes has started to bring its residents together to learn about different home owner issues, such as yard work and house repair. Voice is also helping residents develop their own leaders who can infuse the community — including the local home owners' association — with a diverse set of low-income voices. "They will be an interesting new voice in the community," predicts Hasz. "Home owners had always been the rich people."

THE MAAs IN THE COMMUNITY

The MAA's participation on the International Homes steering committee ultimately put them on new ground, helping them forge new relationships and learn a new issue area. According to Yimir, "Our own communities are looking at our organizations more respectfully; our own constituency is growing. The community sees this project as part of the process of becoming self-sufficient; as home owners, they can't be harassed by a landlord."

THE FUTURE

Voice has now launched another project to develop cooperative housing in Uptown. This new project will build on the lessons learned through International Homes, and try to address shortcomings, like the lack of African American and Latino representation on the International Homes Steering Committee. This new project includes all the members of the Steering Committee, as well as representatives from an African American church and a Latino social service agency.

AFFORDABLE HOUSING UNITES LATINOS AND AFRICAN AMERICANS

WASHINGTON, DC— *The signs of Arlandria's newcomer influx are everywhere. On Mount Vernon Avenue, which cuts through the area's small "downtown," La Feria Latina sells Salvadoran pastries and "pupusas" up the block from stores displaying ornately-decorated "quinceanera" dresses. Despite the newness of this Latin influence, Arlandria remains what it's always been: home to low-income working people.*

THE MORE THINGS CHANGE

AFTER THE FLOOD

During the fierce segregation of the 1950s and 1960s, most of the residents of Arlandria, a neigborhood in the Northern Virginia suburbs of Washington D.C., were white. Then the legal successes of the Civil Rights movement allowed African Americans to move in. White residents took flight in the 1970s, when the area became predominately African American. By the 1980s, thousands of Salvadorans began to arrive in metropolitan Washington fleeing wartime atrocities and bitter poverty in their country. Many of these newcomers migrated to Arlandria seeking housing they could afford. As developers disrupted and dislocated long-term African American residents, reasonable rents drew in more and more Central Americans and transformed Arlandria into a majority Latino neighborhood.

Until the 1970s suburban Arlandria suffered annual flooding that kept real estate developers out and preserved low rents for families that needed it. Then, in 1982, the Army Corps of Engineers stepped in to fix the problem and developers quickly saw the opportunity to make a profit. In 1979 a group of private real estate developers began to convert Arlandria's modest housing into upscale apartments.

To make way for new, higher-income residents, the developers began to raise rents and evict the predominantly African American tenants, pushing families out and threatening the availability of affordable housing in the area. But the tenants battled back, organizing public protests and taking the developers to court under the Fair Housing Act. While the struggle dragged on, Arlandria experienced a dramatic influx of Central American newcomers who joined in the effort. In the mid-1980s, a diverse group of local activists founded a new community organization called the Tenants Support Committee (TSC).

TENANTS ORGANIZE FOR SUPPORT

The Tenants Support Committee formed in 1986 when developers sent out thirty-day eviction notices to 5,000 African American, Central American, and white tenants. Outraged tenants and nearby neighbors, who had already spent years fighting the developers, joined together to form TSC. TSC's mission was to keep Arlandria an affordable and stable place to live. TSC set out to challenge the developers with grassroots activism such as picket lines, letter-writing campaigns, and appeals to local elected officials. TSC's activism helped take the issues out of the narrow confines of the courtroom and into the community, where residents themselves could shape the options. TSC received its first funding from the local Campaign for Human Development and has continued to receive funding from organizations like the Jewish Fund for Justice and the Peace Development Fund.

SEIZING OPPORTUNITIES

TSC has helped nurture tenants' collective power — both reactive and proactive. For example, tenant activism paved the way for a 1987 court settlement which allowed developers to convert modest housing into luxury apartments with the condition that they preserve one quarter of the units for low-income tenants. TSC officially incorporated in 1989 to continue working with tenants, to monitor and implement the settlement, and to advocate for decent and affordable housing. Then, in 1992, the owner of several local apartment buildings went bankrupt and lost the property when his savings and loan company went under. TSC jumped at the chance to help residents purchase the property collectively as a housing cooperative. TSC began working with housing experts to guide residents through the complex process of forming a cooperative. Local residents who had never dreamed of becoming homeowners received training on how to buy and manage property. The housing cooperative they developed has since become a special project of TSC.

NAME:	TENANTS AND WORKERS SUPPORT COMMITTEE (TWSC)
PARTICIPANTS:	CENTRAL AMERICAN NEWCOMERS, AFRICAN AMERICANS, WHITES
GOAL:	AFFORDABLE HOUSING AND ECONOMIC JUSTICE FOR ARLANDRIA RESIDENTS
OBSERVATION:	PRESERVING DIVERSE PARTICIPATION IS CHALLENGING IN A CHANGING NEIGHBORHOOD
INNOVATION:	DRAWING ON DIVERSITY FOR COLLECTIVE COMMUNITY STRENGTH

PRESERVING DIVERSITY

TSC has mounted an uphill battle to preserve diversity among its members. This is no small challenge in an area where African Americans are moving out and Latinos are moving in. About two-thirds of TSC's 120 members are Salvadoran newcomers. The other third include both white and African American established resident. The current board of directors, elected by the general membership, includes five Salvadoran newcomers, three African Americans, and one established white. TSC conducts its meetings in both English and Spanish and produces an English/Spanish newsletter. TSC also holds occasional community dinners to foster personal relationships in the community.

The diversity of TSC's leadership and membership has helped the group forge ties to the Latino immigrant community, which is often isolated from community initiatives, and reach out to African American residents. The participation of higher-income white board members has also helped TSC interface with local government officials.

Maintaining intergroup interaction remains a challenge. For example, lack of common language is a big divider; although TSC's meetings are "bilingual," most of the discussion is held in Spanish, with the meeting's facilitator working double duty translating as much as possible into English. TSC struggles to overcome negative community sentiment. Jesse Taylor, an African American board member, believes that local media have played a negative role in community relations by "mixing everyone up about each other." Taylor reports that "African Americans in the community think that immigrants are coming in and taking over. They feel like more is being done for 'outsiders.'"

MAKING AN IMPACT

Local attitudes, as well as national and international trends, keep TSC in a never-ending learning process. This process has also had real results. TSC's fairly short history has produced a core group of 50 community leaders who are bound by shared experiences, struggles and commitment and who demand that local government and agencies really listen to the concerns of low-income residents and people of color. TSC has also established a youth group that lobbied successfully for the hiring of the area's first bilingual high school counselor, and spearheaded the drive to end the local community college's practice of charging foreign-born students out-of-state tuition. TSC recently changed its name to the Tenants and Workers Support Committee (TWSC). This change reflects the group's new efforts to strengthen local residents' rights in their workplaces as well as in their homes.

INNOVATIVE HOUSING OFFERS NEW HOPE, NEW INTERACTION

snapshot · snapshot · snapshot

LOS ANGELES, CA— Casa Loma feels different. It isn't just the charming courtyards and brightly decorated common rooms that make this new housing development so pleasant. It's also the warmth and commitment that exude from the staff and residents. Casa Loma opened in 1993 as a housing development aimed at low-income mothers in the Belmont Pico Union area of Los Angeles. For 110 Mexican, Central American, Korean, and African American families, Casa Loma is now home. According to Maura, a newcomer from El Salvador, "You enter here and you feel supported, like a daughter."

Casa Loma is the first project of New Economics for Women, an organization of Latinas founded in 1985 to work on economic development and affordable housing for female-headed families. NEW's members — mostly the children and grandchildren of Mexican immigrants — had roots in the Pico Union area and wanted to "give something back" to what has long been an overwhelmingly immigrant neighborhood. Working with a dedicated and experienced housing consultant, herself a Latina, NEW came up with $18 million — a remarkable mix of funds from numerous local government agencies, as well as corporate and financial support.

From the start, newcomer women have guided the direction of Casa Loma. Even before the development was built, NEW held "focus group" discussions to find out how community residents defined their needs and priorities. The women told NEW everything from how gangs intimidate women street vendors to how important the kitchen is to a home. The result is a housing development with unique design features as well as on-site programs and support services like bilingual, bicultural child care, a boys and girls club, a basic skills learning center, and family and career counseling.

Casa Loma's families continue to shape its direction through the Resident Council. At Resident Council meetings, which are held in Spanish with volunteers providing Korean and English interpretation, residents make decisions about how the center is run, plan fund-raisers and activities, and voice concerns. Casa Loma residents recently discussed the interpersonal tensions that had arisen between some Mexican and Central American women. According to Sandra Villalobos, Casa Loma's project director, the issues were small but important, "like whether to serve Salvadoran *pupusas* or Mexican *guacamole*." The residents decided that they needed "resident facilitators" from each race and nationality who could intervene in tense situations and voted to bring in a conflict resolution trainer from San Francisco to help them develop their approach.

COMMUNITY INNOVATIONS:
ECONOMIC STRATEGIES

CREDIT UNION BUILDS ECONOMIC TIES

NEW YORK, NY— *Take the "F" train from Manhattan, get off at the Fulton Street station and you'll find yourself in the vibrant and bustling heart of Central Brooklyn. Fulton Street itself is jammed with families, street vendors and livery cab drivers — virtually all of them Black, many of them newcomers. Central Brooklyn — better known by its geographic parts such as Crown Heights, Bedford-Stuyvesant, Fort Greene, Prospect Heights, and East Flatbush — is the largest contiguous Black community in the nation.*

TAKE THE "F" TRAIN

Central Brooklyn is home to generations of African Americans and large numbers of newcomers from Jamaica, Haiti, Trinidad, and the Dominican Republic. Families matter a lot here, as do community organizations, churches, and political leaders who often belong to one nationality or another. Race unites and distinguishes area residents, but tensions sometimes flare up between people of different nationalities. Sometimes different groups compete for resources; often they work in isolation. Sometimes, there is a compelling reason to work together, as in the case of Fulton Street's Central Brooklyn Federal Credit Union.

TAKING ECONOMIC CONTROL

New York would come to a screeching halt without the service sector workers — food preparers, janitors, security guards — who live in areas like Central Brooklyn. But Central Brooklyn's own residents struggle to maintain a secure economic base. In 1988 this struggle sparked the tiny Crown Heights Neighborhood Improvement Association which started to call together different community organizations to decide what kind of economic development they wanted to see. What they wanted were financial resources that residents could use to start businesses and develop affordable housing. What they needed was access to loans and funding directed by the community instead of by city agencies.

Nobody funded this consensus-building process, but the Association was able to provide support in the form of staffer Mark Griffith, a first-generation Jamaican who grew up in the area and returned after time away in the Ivy League and Africa. "We all recognized the need for another kind of development," recalls Griffith, who was only 26 at the time. The group decided to establish a locally based credit union and an economic development coalition, "so whatever we did was in the name of the entire community." In 1989, these groups formed the Central Brooklyn Partnership with Griffith as the director.

A Board that Transcends Differences

Bringing together organizations representing different nationalities was key to the Partnership's strategy. "We believed that the overwhelming need for economic development should transcend petty differences [between groups] .... We need to work on our own self-direction rather than scapegoating immigrants," says Patrick Hilton, a Haitian-born community leader and credit union board member. "We wanted all the [Caribbean] islands represented on the board," says credit union co-founder Erol Louis, "combined with an understanding of what the long-established black community has been through." This commitment has produced a board that currently includes leaders from the Jamaican, Dominican, Haitian, and African American communities.

Name:	**Central Brooklyn Federal Credit Union**
Participants:	**Caribbean and African newcomers, African Americans**
Goal:	**A broadly supported, self-generated economic base for the community**
Observation:	**Black communities are forging newcomer/established resident collaboration**
Innovation:	**Building economic development based on cultural identities**

Building Community Support

The Partnership worked hard to nurture community support and investments in the credit union. This meant understanding Central Brooklyn's different cultures and working with their institutions. Credit union supporters used grassroots outreach, such as visits to churches and card tables at block parties, to convince 1,600 individuals to "pledge" a deposit to the credit union, thus ensuring that the union would meet federal requirements. Supporters also pointed to residents' own cultural experiences, such as the Caribbean economic collective known as a "sou-sous," to explain the credit union concept. They appealed to community leaders to reach out to very recent newcomers who make a vital contribution to the area's economy but are often isolated by language and cultural barriers.

Finding Other Resources

Support from outside the community was also badly needed. The Partnership itself started out with no funds, then got a subsistence grant from the Northstar Fund. The National Association of Community Development Credit Unions provided non-monetary support to the Partnership, such as free technical assistance and volunteer researchers who discovered that for every dollar of deposits large banks received from the community, only one penny was put back into the community in the form of home loans. The Partnership also took advantage of the VISTA volunteer program to secure much-needed staff. It wasn't until 1992 that the Partnership received its first significant funding, a grant from the New York Foundation. Finally, the Partnership was able to get loans from commercial banks by leveraging pressure through the Community Reinvestment Act (CRA), a law which helps community groups get support from banks that have failed to lend in poor communities.

In May 1993, the Central Brooklyn Federal Community Development Credit Union finally opened its doors. In its first year, it lent out $150,000 in loans to individuals and $130,000 in loans to businesses. Each loan is very small — one secured by an African American woman was used to buy a computer program to keep her tax preparation service afloat.

KEEP BUILDING

Mark Griffith acknowledges that the Partnership and the credit union can do a lot more

to bring different people together. He recently began working with a Haitian volunteer to increase the credit union's outreach in the Haitian community. The credit union has also pioneered interaction with the area's Muslim members, who are forbidden by Islamic law to receive interest on their savings: the credit union developed special non-interest accounts for the Muslims, bringing them into the credit union membership and bridging an important community gap. "We also have to make a conscious effort to make loans to non-Carribbeans," says Griffith, "so we represent a diverse group." Griffith believes that "economic development brings people together in the natural arena where things happen. We need to build economic structures that benefit both immigrants and non-immigrants."

"We believed that the overwhelming need for economic development should transcend petty differences [between groups] .... We need to work on our own self-direction rather than scapegoating immigrants."

JANITORS SEEK RESPECT AND UNITY

WASHINGTON, DC— *"Employers don't hire blacks as janitors," says Lindolfo Carballo, speaking in Spanish. "They tell blacks there's no work, then they hire Latinos. When we [the union] accused them of discrimination, they hired a few." Carballo, a Salvadoran newcomer and union organizer, shakes his head. "Latinos don't want to take jobs away from blacks. The companies try to separate and divide us. But if there are blacks and Latinos working together, the potential for discrimination goes down."*

SEPARATING & DIVIDING

LEARNING TO WORK TOGETHER

In 1991, Washington janitors gained an unprecedented, united voice for their cause. That year, Local 82, the predominantly African American government janitors' union, merged with Justice for Janitors union Local 525, the predominantly Latino commercial janitors' union. This merger reflected a new organizing movement among America's growing number of service sector workers. Immigrants around the country are infusing service sector labor unions with new energy and new challenges, struggling alongside established residents to ensure that everyone can earn a decent living. Within Local 82/Justice for Janitors, union members and staff are learning to work together across race and ethnic lines to achieve their goals.

GETTING ORGANIZED

Local 82/Justice for Janitors' mission is to organize janitors for good wages, decent treatment, health benefits, and protection against forced part-time work, as well as to change public policies that affect janitors and other service sector workers. The union is targeting the practices of private companies who offer janitorial services on contract to building owners. These contractors often deny employees the right to organize, pay workers wages well below the national average, and violate labor, health, and safety laws. When a building owner takes on a new contractor — something which happens quite frequently — that contractor often fires the janitors already working in the building.

Local 82, a member of the Service Employees International Union (SEIU), started out representing both government and commercial janitors, most of whom were African American. However, when contracting companies joined together in the 1970s to block any demands for higher wages, commercial janitors' organizing efforts became paralyzed and Local 82 narrowed its focus to janitors employed directly by the government.

Commercial janitors remained largely unorganized until the mid-1980s when the SEIU launched its nationwide Justice for Janitors campaign, an attempt to organize commercial sector janitors. Justice for Janitors targeted Washington, D.C. for one of its major efforts. The current president of Local 82, an African American named Mary Martin, says she supported the merger because "it would make all of us stronger." In many ways, her hope has been realized.

GRASSROOTS INTERACTION

Without the union, Latino and African American janitors would have had little chance to interact. Most of Washington's commercial janitors are Latino newcomers, whose language and immigration status make them less likely than established residents to challenge questionable employer practices. Although African Americans also work as commercial janitors, employers rarely put Latinos and African Americans to work in the same building. Most of Washington's government janitors are African Americans, who enjoy fewer employment options than other Americans, but do not face the language and legal status barriers of newcomers. The workplace "segregation" of African American and Latino janitors makes the union one of the few places they can come together.

NAME:	**LOCAL 82/JUSTICE FOR JANITORS**
PARTICIPANTS:	**CENTRAL AMERICAN NEWCOMERS, AFRICAN AMERICANS**
GOAL:	**DECENT WAGES AND WORK CONDITIONS, AND PUBLIC POLICIES THAT PROTECT ALL WORKERS**
OBSERVATION:	**UNITY OF MISSION IS NECESSARY, BUT NOT SUFFICIENT, FOR BUILDING STRONG INDIVIDUAL RELATIONSHIPS**
INNOVATION:	**BUILDING AN ORGANIZATION IN WHICH NEWCOMER AND ESTABLISHED AMERICAN WORKERS CAN BAND TOGETHER TO ADDRESS WORKPLACE EXPLOITATION**

Meetings, picket lines, and demonstrations offer janitors a chance to work together. African American and Latino union members attend meetings together where they make collective decisions about worker benefits and priority concerns. At these meetings, a bilingual union employee sits up front. English speakers talk, then pause while the interpreter repeats their words in Spanish. Spanish speakers also make comments and ask questions which the interpreter restates in English.

The union also gives African American and Latino janitors a chance to advocate together for improvements in the workplace. Recently, African American and Latino union members succeeded in calling attention to the kind of discrimination which so worries organizer Lindolfo Carballo. The union gathered information from African American and Latino janitors who charged that a local janitorial service company was refusing to hire African Americans. Government and commercial janitors then held joint demonstrations protesting the company's practices. The union's legal and grassroots strategy sparked an investigation by the Equal Employment Opportunity Commission (EEOC), which may help ensure that all workers are protected against discrimination.

Latinos and African Americans also have a chance to work together as leaders. The decision-making board of Local 82/Justice for Janitors is made up of a representative from each organized building. This board includes Latinos, African Americans, and whites, reflecting the racial and ethnic diversity of the membership.

Both African Americans and Latinos insist that few tensions exist between the two groups of members. According to both, the biggest challenge is making sure that each group is able to participate actively in the union. For example, getting Latinos and African Americans on the same schedule is itself

When the merger of the two unions took place "we were too busy to think about race and ethnic relations."

a hurdle. "It's hard for the Latinos to meet on Saturday because so many of them have second jobs," says Mary Martin. "It's also hard for them to participate because they don't speak English and don't know union procedures. And a lot of them have small children." Latinos and African Americans still tend to cluster together in groups at membership meetings, and interpreters sometimes forget to translate questions and answers in addition to presentations, but the meetings attract solid numbers of both groups, and the quality of communication at these meetings remains remarkably high.

A Second Look at Staff Interaction

Local 82 staff and Justice for Janitors staff have hit some unexpected bumps over the years. Reflecting the membership of the union, most of the Local 82 staff have been African American while most of the Justice for Janitors staff have been Latino. Nonetheless, Mary Martin recalls that when the merger of the two unions took place "we were too busy to think about [race and ethnic relations]." Since then, the two groups have worked on different floors and have had different agendas: Local 82 staff focus on services and benefits for federal members, while Justice for Janitors staff focus on recruiting commercial janitors to join the union. Local 82 staff speak to each other in English while Justice for Janitors staff communicate in Spanish. Staff members from the two groups have co-existed, but with little opportunity to work on collaborative projects. Now, both African American and Latino staff report that issues between individuals from both groups are more and more likely to become racialized, and that misunderstanding and resentment between the two groups needs attention. Three years after the merger, Local 82/Justice for Janitors has begun to consider ways to build staff relationships that parallel the remarkable unity they have forged for others. Martin believes that the challenges are worth it because the merger has been a "positive event" which "got people involved in things they hadn't before: a lot of activity, learning something new."

THE EFFECTIVENESS OF UNITY

Local 82/Justice for Janitors continues to grow in size and influence. Twenty five hundred new members signed up between 1989 and 1993, doubling the overall membership and increasing the union's financial resources. The union has provided support to individual members, such as the recent case of a janitor who sought to have his employer pay his medical expenses for an on-the-job injury. The union's advocacy efforts also helped bring passage of the city's new "Displaced Workers Protection Act," which helps protect janitors' jobs when a building owner changes contractors, and offers new protections for the many "invisible" workers on whom cities like Washington, D.C. depend.

STREET VENDORS STRUGGLE FOR LIVELIHOOD AND UNITY

LOS ANGELES, CA — The Sidewalk Vendors Coalition of Los Angeles is a new effort to unify street vending's diverse proponents around a concrete economic development plan. Until very recently, most street vending was illegal in Los Angeles, punishable by six months in jail or a $1,000 fine. This prohibition did little to stop thousands of people from peddling t-shirts, fruit, and cassettes to make ends meet. When street vending boomed in the 1980s, police began to crack down. In the first six months of 1990, they arrested more than 2,000 vendors. After years of heated debate among opponents and proponents of legalized street vending, the Los Angeles City Council passed legislation in 1993 designed to appease both parties. The new legislation created a two-year pilot program which allowed for the creation of eight legal street-vending "districts."

The fight for legalized street vending began with the street vendors themselves. In 1986 the Central American Resource Center (CARECEN) helped street vendors in the Latino immigrant neighborhood of Pico Union organize into an Asociacion de Vendedores Ambulantes (AVA). AVA members, mostly single mothers, wanted to stop what they saw as police harassment of them. AVA worked with others, such as immigrant advocates, who argue that resistance to legalized vending reflects anti-immigrant sentiment, and public officials like Los Angeles City Councilman Mike Hernandez who believes that "street vending is the purest form of economic development. Denying people the opportunity to contribute to the fabric that is Los Angeles also makes no sense."

At first the media — and supporters of street vending — saw this as strictly a Latino issue. Soon, though, a handful of African Americans began to speak out in favor of street vending as a way to revitalize their own communities. Ezekiel Mobley was the first African American to join the coalition, working on behalf of the African Marketplace, an annual vendors fair. "It may have been an eye opener for the group," says Mobley. Anthony Scott, African American director of the Dunbar Economic Development Corporation, joined the coalition to represent the concerns of street vendors in South Central. AVA itself discovered a tiny African American vendors association in Watts and began working with them, as well, to call attention to the issue. "The street vending issue is a question of what we are going to do as groups in this geographic area," argues Mobley, "of not waiting for forces to throw us together. We need to try to anticipate the economic landscape. There are some potential collaborations between immigrants and African Americans that are really meaningful."

Although the City Council has approved the development of legal street vending districts, the new law makes it very difficult to establish a district and very expensive for vendors to become licensed within a district. The coalition therefore created the PASEO Program (Pedestrian Areas for Shopping and Economic Opportunity) to guide sidewalk vendors through the process and to bring vendors together with other members of the community around the goal of economic revitalization. According to Alison Leigh Becker, Coalition Coordinator, "we hope to get people to talk to each other around common problems." This won't be easy. In Los Angeles, as in cities across the country, opponents of legalized vending have included storeowners — sometimes the children of immigrants — who believe street vending threatens their livelihood, property owners and developers, many of whom are white, who believe street vending contributes to urban decay, and some African American leaders, who believe that street vending is an immigrant issue that should take a back seat to other, long-standing community concerns. On sidewalks across the country, street vending has become an economic and political struggle that touches the raw nerves of race, ethnic, and class relations.

LOAN FUND ATTRACTS DIVERSE ENTREPRENEURS

WASHINGTON, DC— Pricilla is from Cameroon and sells greeting cards she makes herself. Audrey grew up in Washington, DC and has just started a housecleaning service. Both are members of the 500 Club, a small group of grassroots entrepreneurs working together to get off the ground. All of the 500 Club members are Black, yet they represent a broad cultural mix of African Americans and newcomers from Nigeria, Cameroon, and Panama. "I never really had different culture friends until I came here," says Audrey. Pricilla agrees, "Now Audrey's just like a childhood friend. That's what you miss from home. That's what you miss in America."

The 500 Club is part of the recently established Barnabus Self-Employment Fund, a loan fund and training program that helps low-income residents start their own businesses. Each participant in the Barnabus Fund becomes a member of a business loan group, a small circle of people who train together and take collective responsibility for the loans each receives. The Barnabus Fund was established in 1993 by Jubilee Jobs, a community agency that has been providing free employment counseling and placements to Washington residents for the last twelve years. More and more often, job counselors were finding that jobs available to their clients did not pay a survival wage and that clients needed new ways to augment their income.

The Barnabus Fund has built on Jubilee Jobs' experience working with newcomers and established residents, seeking ways to bring people from different backgrounds together. Members of the 500 Club range from an African American man offering bicycle repairs to a Liberian woman selling women's accessories. Participants believe this interaction has changed them. "I'm more outgoing in the street," says Audrey. "I can relate better to other nationalities. But it took me to come here to really be able to."

In its first year, the Barnabus Fund provided training to 63 people. The Fund's first loan, $500 for a sidewalk vending business, has already been repaid, and loans for other ventures, such as one extended to a bronzing business, are being considered. A "funders club" of individual donors supports the Fund, as do local foundations and religious organizations.

Tony Cauterruci, the Fund's director, speaks candidly of the challenges involved in bringing diverse groups together. Outreach programs and scheduling group meetings, for instance, have been a challenge. His efforts have been largely successful. The Fund is currently developing "savings clubs" to bring in already existing groups, such as sewing circles or church groups. The Fund has established a Spanish-only training and loan group and Cauterruci also intends to bring other participants together for training on cross-cutting issues. The Fund hopes to increase the numbers and diversity of its participants by working with other community organizations and placing advertisements in the local African American and Latino newspapers.

Jewish Group Leads Business Outreach Network

New York, NY— Communities where newcomers and established residents live often depend on "mom and pop" businesses for jobs. Unfortunately, these small businesses frequently face culture, language, and class barriers that prevent them from getting assistance and services to stay afloat. A Jewish organization in New York is working throughout the region in an effort to foster small business development.

In 1993 the Council of Jewish Organizations (COJO) of Boro Park, Brooklyn decided it was time to reach out beyond its own neighborhood of Orthodox Jews and Russian and European newcomers. That year COJO launched the Business Outreach Center (BOC) Network to help already-established community institutions provide local businesses with information and guidance regarding loans, skills, and training, and to help them share technology and resources across geographic and cultural boundaries.

BOC's Network currently includes organizations like the Church Avenue Merchants Block Association (CAMBA) in Flatbush, Brooklyn, home to Asians, Carribbeans, African Americans, and Latinos, and the Chinatown Manpower Project, which works in collaboration with the South Manhattan Development Corporation in the predominantly Latino Lower East Side. "We're trying to blend a community-based approach with regional strength," says John Fratianni, who heads BOC's network services. "It means a real change in philosophy and approach."

The BOC Network has also meant new relationships. When Elvis Herrera of the Hunts Point, Bronx BOC was invited to help a local utility reach out to small businesses in the community, he was shocked to find that no one had been asked to represent the Bronx's more than 2,500 Korean businesses. Herrera quickly worked through his network contacts to find a Korean business leader who could serve as an advisor to the utility. Since then, Herrera and BOC have worked to bring Korean small business owners into contact with other businesses and organizations throughout the metropolitan area.

BOC recently formed a remarkable new partnership with an African American Muslim organization. In the summer of 1994, the BOC Network added the Harlem Business Outreach Center, run by the Masjid Malcolm Shabazz. "It's been very exciting to see both the leaders and staff members of an Orthodox/Hasidic Jewish organization working together with African American Muslims," says Nancy Carin, BOC Network Director. "Both groups are socially conservative and committed to self-help. They found they had a lot more in common than they thought."

INTERNATIONAL MARKET HIGHLIGHTS SUBURBAN DIVERSITY

WASHINGTON, DC— At the Clarendon International Market, suburban shoppers browse through Thai, Mexican, and Native-American jewelry, peruse Japanese and American literature, see Bolivian art and enjoy Chinese and African food — all within sixty outside booths in the parking lot of a former Sears Automotive Center. The Clarendon International Market, located in Northern Virginia, brings together artists, merchants, and craftspeople from the local area as well as countries such as Poland, Vietnam, India, Guatemala, Korea and Ghana. The Clarendon Alliance, which sponsors the International Market, hopes to promote economic development and investment in the local community while providing artists with a steady physical location to display and sell their wares. The creation of the marketplace was a real opportunity for the vendors, many of whom had little ability to market their crafts without the marketplace.

The Market receives funding through the Neighborhood Partnership Fund of the Arlington Community Foundation, a project aimed at providing financial support to community-based initiatives which increase interaction between foreign-born and native residents. In developing the Fund, the Arlington Community Foundation went out of its way to find dynamic new local leaders who could point them toward innovations taking place in the community. The Fund provides support to any community group based in Arlington which brings together ethnically diverse neighbors or that helps the newcomers become self-sustaining.

COMMUNITY INNOVATIONS:

EDUCATION AND LEADERSHIP

FAMILY LITERACY PROGRAM LINKS NEW AND OLD

CHICAGO, IL— At mid-day in August the halls of the ALBA Homes Community Center feel empty. But in Almita Rushell's tiny classroom a dozen African American women, a few with toddlers in tow, cluster cozily around a table. The women are looking intently at their workbooks as Almita's warm enthusiastic voice gently prods them. "Can anyone sound that word out? Does it look like any other word you've seen?" A few miles south in Chicago's Pilsen neighborhood, a group of Mexican immigrant women sit in a circle of chairs in Casa Atzlan's large meeting room. A few children giggle and play in the open space in the middle of the room. The women work together on a survey form, in English and in Spanish, asking their opinions about the possible closing of a nearby open-air market.

Although these two literacy classes take place only a few miles apart, the distance between them can seem vast. Since 1992, however, the Multicultural Family Literacy Program has been bringing these African American and Latino students together twice a month to discuss common community issues and concerns. Before that, the women report, the only chance African American and Latina women had to interact was while shopping.

Cynthia Chico-Rodriguez, former director of the Casa Atzlan community center, remembers how she began to see literacy as an issue in both communities. "We really started to think about the connection when African American women and their children started coming to our hot meals program. When they'd ask about adult education we'd refer them to other programs. But it got us thinking."

The Multicultural Family Literacy Program involves approximately 30 students—15 from Casa Aztlan and 15 from ALBA homes. Participants sign up for the program knowing they will interact with women of a different race or ethnicity. The program includes activities designed to bring African Americans and Latinos together, such as a panel discussion on women's issues, which also attracted an audience beyond the program's immediate participants, and an oral book report which drew 70 people. "This program empowers people where they are. Everybody wants to see everybody as distant," says Almita Russell, the coordinator of the literacy program for the ALBA Homes housing project. "This program gives residents an opportunity to get outside their own community and think about what they'd want to change. This program has made African American and Latino women closer and more aware." A Mexican American women in the program agrees. "We want to meet," she says in Spanish. "It's a process that takes time; but we're trying."

LEADERSHIP PROGRAM BUILDS INTERGROUP TRUST

LOS ANGELES, CA— In January 1991, The Asian Pacific American Legal Center of Southern California (APALC) initiated a program like no other in California — a program designed to bring together potential leaders from different ethnic groups to focus on a specific community project. Leadership Development in Interethnic Relations (LDIR), a nine-month leadership training program, draws multi-ethnic community leaders from three geographic locations in Southern California (West San Gabriel Valley, Koreatown/South Central Los Angeles and Gardena/South Bay). While APALC was initially responsible for getting the program off and running, they were later joined in their efforts by the League of United Latin American Citizens (LULAC) and the Martin Luther King Dispute Resolution Center (MLKDRC) of the Southern Christian Leadership Conference (SCLC).

LIDR uses cultural awareness methods as well as skills building in conflict resolution and community organizing. The program teaches community leaders how to establish common ground with leaders from other communities and come together to improve community relations and challenge racial and social stereotypes. Prosy Abarquez-Delacruz, a Filipina and one of the LIDR's first graduates, believes that the program "takes immigrants out of their comfort zone in order to deal with non-immigrants."

COMMUNITY INNOVATIONS:

NEIGHBORHOOD ADVOCACY

RELATIONSHIPS ARE GLUE FOR 'ORGANIZATION OF ORGANIZATIONS'

CHICAGO, IL — *Most people agree that individual relationships are the glue that holds an organization together. But how many organizations care enough about that glue to conduct one-on-one interviews with 50 people in their community? One hundred? In Chicago's Uptown/Edgewater area, the Organization of the NorthEast (ONE) went that far — and further, conducting over 400 individual interviews over the course of just one year. ONE then used what it had learned to build an "organization of organizations" in one of the most diverse neighborhoods in the country.*

FOUR HUNDRED INTERVIEWS

MELDING FRAGMENTS

Josh Hoyt had years of community organizing under his belt when he took over as Executive Director of ONE in 1990. Hoyt had trained with the Industrial Areas Foundation (IAF), a fifty-year-old community organizing network built on the principle of one-on-one relationships. He had learned the hard way that nothing gets done without strong, honest personal relationships. Hoyt had also learned that no white guy could drop into a multiethnic, multiracial community and tell folks what needed to be done. What he could do was ask himself and others to take a hard look at themselves and their community, and build a vision that was both real and daring. In 1990 Hoyt and his "co-conspirators" set out to harness the energy of an astoundingly diverse neighborhood and to reinvigorate a decades-old organization that most residents no longer saw as useful.

Hoyt began talking to people in Uptown/Edgewater, and found a small circle who believed that the community's ethnic and economic diversity was an opportunity being squandered. These community residents believed that organizations representing different racial and ethnic groups had no common place to discuss their concerns about the community and their ideas for improving it. Community activists often had little contact with the immigrant business associations or small ethnic organizations that residents turned to for leadership. Moreover, each local organization had its own agenda and projects, sometimes duplicating the efforts of another organization up the block. What Hoyt and others saw was fragmentation. What they created was a new ONE that could meld these fragments together building power and bringing new resources to the area.

TALKING, EATING, ARGUING, PLANNING

The process of rebuilding ONE was straightforward but time-consuming: meet people, find out their concerns, and get them talking to each other. "Our approach was 'relational,'" says Hoyt, referring to the interviews ONE's members, board, and staff conducted with community leaders. ONE met individually or in small groups with community leaders, listening to their ideas and concerns and establishing personal relationships.

ONE then sponsored a series of community dinner/dialogues to pull these individual leaders together. Each dinner attracted more than one hundred people from over forty different community institutions. Each evening focused on one of the major themes that had emerged from the interviews: community, family, and vision. After dinner a guest speaker made a presentation and attempted to stir up discussion. Participants at each table shared their views on community problems, opportunities, and priorities for action. For many, the small group discussions were the first interaction they had had with people outside their familiar circle. This interaction was sometimes difficult, recalls Sue Ellen Long, a member of the Uptown/Edgewater Chamber of Commerce and an Organization of the NorthEast board member recruited by Hoyt: "Josh's approach to tensions was to try to bring them out, get people fighting openly with each other. He diffused tension by communicating, getting facts." Another ONE board member, Dr. Joaquim Villegas, credits this approach with transforming the organization into a "catalyst for different racial and ethnic groups to focus on key issues collaboratively."

NAME:	**ORGANIZATION OF THE NORTHEAST (ONE)**
PARTICIPANTS:	**ASIAN, EASTERN EUROPEAN AND LATIN AMERICAN NEWCOMERS, AFRICAN AMERICANS AND WHITES**
GOAL:	**A SUCCESSFUL MULTIETHNIC, MIXED-ECONOMIC COMMUNITY**
OBSERVATION:	**INDIVIDUAL RELATIONSHIPS ARE THE FOUNDATION FOR COMMUNITY CHANGE**
INNOVATION:	**INVESTING IN INDIVIDUAL RELATIONSHIPS — WHICH INCLUDES AIRING TENSIONS — TO CREATE A UNITED, EFFECTIVE COMMUNITY VOICE**

NOT AN AIMLESS JOURNEY

Power and strategic focus were also on each evening's agenda. According to Long, "the 'glue' that brought people together was the desire to be part of a bigger group and have more clout. ONE was the vehicle for getting results." Focus was also key. As Reverend Paul Koch, President of ONE's board, told the participants at one dinner, "This is not an aimless, accidental journey, a wilderness meandering, but an intentional journey" to build a powerful and diverse Uptown/Edgewater. By the end of the three dinners, participants had selected four community challenges they wanted to work on: housing, crime, education, and cultural diversity. This agenda, and the energy of the people behind it, became the foundation for the new ONE.

AN ORGANIZATION OF ORGANIZATIONS

The new ONE became an "organization of organizations" — forty-two community institutions that shared the goal of building a successful multiethnic, mixed-income community. Today, ONE's membership consists of 59 institutions including tenant associations and housing development groups, banks, colleges, alternative schools, unions, ethnic organizations, and social services agencies. Members pay dues that now total more than $50,000. ONE gets the rest of its funds from the United Way and other foundations. The organization does not accept government funds.

ONE met individually or in small groups with community leaders, listening to their ideas and concerns and establishing personal relationships.

ONE holds a convention each year which attracts from 500 to 1,400 delegates from the community. Convention delegates set the basic direction for ONE's efforts in the coming year and elect ONE's Board of Directors. Political officials — like the Mayor and Members of Congress — also attend, giving delegates a chance to urge support for ONE's agenda. During the year, ONE members work in three "strategy teams," each of which focuses on how to meet concrete goals in the areas of jobs/economic development, youth/family/education, and housing. The strategy teams present their plans at a bi-monthly Action Council meeting, in which members make decisions that will have an immediate and measurable impact. The Action Council meetings ensure that people receive acknowledgment for their hard work and that they are held accountable for achieving their stated goals.

A HISTORY OF SUCCESS

ONE has succeeded in bringing both power and resources to Uptown/Edgewater. In the past five years, ONE has helped to bring in $50,000 for three local tenant associations and has secured a half million dollars in federal grants to help 1,000 local students get special school-to-work training. In addition, ONE has helped members to shape public policy positions and develop strategies for attracting the attention of candidates for public office. At the same time, the organization remains committed to the most basic grassroots interaction, such as organizing a science club for young people and a Family Science Night to stimulate enthusiasm for the subject.

No Rest for the Weary

Despite its success, ONE must continually revise and regroup. "Success" once meant just surviving as an organization. Now ONE must find ways to expand its creativity and power. This means taking on new issues and problems. It also means rekindling active member participation all the time — honestly assessing what's working, ripping down what isn't, and rebuilding again. For an organization based on individual relationships, there's never a dull moment.

African Americans and Latinos Fight Liquor Store Proliferation

Los Angeles, CA — *Around the corner from the grit of Broadway Street, modest homes, tidy gardens, and freshly-mowed squares of lawn evoke memories of South Central from a different time. For decades, African American families predominated here, taking pride in their work for manufacturing plants like B.F. Goodrich and U.S. Steel. Back then, no one could have imagined the shock that was to come. One by one, beginning in the 1970s, the companies which had once thrived on South Central's labor closed their doors and left. Hundreds of thousands of jobs vanished forever.*

South Central, 1994

Many African American families moved out to find jobs elsewhere. Others, particularly senior citizens, stayed put as newcomer Mexican and Central American families repopulated South Central's neighborhoods. Korean newcomers also came to the area, not to live but to buy small corner stores, work hard, and invest their pooled family resources. By the 1990s, Latinos made up half of South Central's population and Asians owned a majority of its liquor stores.

A Symbol of Decline

Liquor stores had been a troublesome issue long before the Community Coalition for Substance Abuse opened its doors in 1990. By then, many of South Central's residents had come to believe there were just too many liquor stores. Others had become fearful and angry because of the crime and violence that some liquor stores attracted. One liquor store had been the site of so many incidents that the police had dubbed it the "Bucket of Blood." For South Central's African American residents and their newer Latino neighbors, corner liquor stores symbolized a community in trouble. Some South Central residents also resented the fact that so many liquor store owners were Korean newcomers — a theme the media often emphasized.

Stop Them From Coming Back

The "Campaign to Rebuild South Central Without Problem Liquor Stores" began on June 20, 1992, one month after the acquittal of the police officers accused of beating Rodney King and the ensuing urban violence. In three days, 200 liquor stores in South Central had been partially or completely burned down. Residents of South Central were shocked and horrified by the chaos, but some saw the potential for change. These residents turned to the Coalition. "Our phone started ringing off the hook with people saying `Stop these stores from coming back'," recalls Silvia Castillo, a Mexican American member of the Coalition staff. "There was a spontaneous outpouring. We knew we would need to organize and direct this emotional upheaval. We had to completely revise our strategy."

The Coalition, led by an African American woman named Karen Bass, believed that this new strategy should be a grassroots collaboration between African American and Latino residents who seldom worked together. Bass and Castillo also believed that this grassroots collaboration should build on the dignity and power of area residents, not on hostility toward Asian newcomers (See box: "A Principled Response; p. 65).

A NEW SITUATION; A NEW STRATEGY

The Coalition found direction in the organizing efforts they had already begun. Castillo and Bass had started mobilizing residents to challenge the liquor licenses of owners whose stores were linked with crime and substance abuse. In fact, the night before the 1992 disturbances, a Coalition meeting on the issue had attracted 150 African American and Latino residents, as well as representatives from the City Council and Mayor's Office. After the riots, however the Coalition needed to rethink its whole approach.

NAME:	CAMPAIGN TO REBUILD SOUTH CENTRAL WITHOUT PROBLEM LIQUOR STORES
PARTICIPANTS:	AFRICAN AMERICANS, LATINOS
GOAL:	ELIMINATE PROBLEM LIQUOR STORES FROM COMMUNITY
INNOVATION:	FACILITATING GRASSROOTS COLLABORATION AMONG AFRICAN AMERICANS AND LATINOS WITHOUT ENCOURAGING ANTI-ASIAN SENTIMENT

STARTING TO ORGANIZE

On April 28, 150 African American and Latino residents showed up for the Coalition's first community meeting on the liquor store problem. The Coalition had already done its homework: their community survey, conducted by African American senior citizens, had found 728 liquor licenses in South Central, as many as existed in the entire state of Rhode Island. The City Council member and staff from the Mayor's office were impressed and promised closer scrutiny of the area's liquor stores.

The foundation of this new strategy was set when the city passed the "Emergency Rebuild" ordinance which strengthened local resident power. This ordinance created a public hearing process for the rebuilding of "sensitive land uses," such as liquor stores, and gave the city the power to impose restrictions on the rebuilding. The Campaign set out to educate residents about how they could use the "Emergency Rebuild" ordinance to influence the rebuilding process and to mobilize them to demand policies that would give residents more control over their neighborhoods. The Campaign took direct, grassroots action like canvassing door-to-door, holding community meetings with elected officials, and organizing public rallies. The Campaign also sought out the donated services of

Bass and Castillo had always known they were treading onto a race relations mine field. When they began the Campaign, the two community leaders reconnected with Asian leaders they had worked with in the past. Bong Hwan Kim was one such leader. Kim, director of the Korean Youth and Community Center (KYCC), was a well-respected community leader who had co-chaired the defunct Black/Korean Alliance, an effort to improve relations between African American customers and Korean shopkeepers. Kim was eager to help squelch anti-Asian sentiment among liquor store opponents. Bass and Castillo met with Kim and others, putting the problem in blunt terms: "We said 'Here's what we're going to do. Can we work together so the mission is clear and doesn't become racialized?'" What resulted from these discussions was the Alliance for Neighborhood Economic Development, a collaborative project to help liquor store owners convert to other forms of business.

Just talking about such conversion took guts. With newspaper headlines screaming about hostilities between Koreans and African Americans, the rebuilding of liquor stores after the Los Angeles riots became one of the most highly publicized intergroup conflicts in the country. For Korean families who lost everything in the fires, and who received little if any emergency assistance, the need to rebuild was desperate. At the same time, African American and Latino communities urgently needed a way to control the downward spiral of their neighborhoods. Beneath the painfully real concerns of both groups lay mistrust and animosity that had festered for years. "Conflict resolution per se wasn't going to work," says Deborah Ching of the Chinatown Service Center and President of the Asian Pacific Planning Council (APPCON), a coalition of Asian organizations. What was needed was an innovative way to help store owners regain their livelihood and set up businesses that communities want and need.

The Alliance was officially launched at a press conference on May 28, 1993. The Alliance's initial goal was to convert 30 liquor stores from the more than 300 that had been destroyed in the unrest. The program provides individual business counseling as well as entrepreneurial skills training, support services, and access to capital. The Alliance receives local government funding and private support including grants from the California Wellness Foundation and Bank of America. The Alliance's accomplishments have been modest but impressive. In a year and a half, three liquor stores have gone through the long and challenging process

A PRINCIPLED RESPONSE

of transformation. Two converted to laundromats; the third became part of a mini-mall development that now includes a donut shop and a medical clinic. These efforts may seem small by some standards, but in neighborhoods where jobs and capital are painfully hard to come by, no success is taken for granted. These three conversions keep at least 30 people employed and offer distressed areas an economic and psychological shot in the arm. "African American community residents have been overwhelmed when they've seen that we really did it," says Pat Wong, Alliance director. "We've also overcome a lot of skepticism from the Korean community."

The future of the Alliance depends largely on funding. Monies that became available after the 1992 unrest have now dried up, leaving more projects competing for fewer resources. Supporters of the Alliance may be disappointed, but they have always recognized the enormity of the task. According to Erick Nakano of the Little Tokyo Service Center, the project "just scratches the surface of a lot of issues. Tensions between African Americans and Asians are very complicated." But Nakano still believes that the project "represents one of the few principled attempts at problem-solving. We're trying to focus on justice, fairness, and mutual self-interest. The basic issues are economic — all the `multicultural' stuff won't solve that."

lawyers and other experts who could guide them through the maze of legislation, hearings, and court battles that lay ahead.

One of the Campaign's first efforts was a petition drive calling for the city to prevent the reopening of problem liquor stores. Volunteers collected 7,500 signatures in one month. An August community meeting with the Mayor drew 350 people. When the Coalition called for a demonstration in the state capital, nearly 150 South Central residents made the eight-hour trek.

RESIDENT UNITY

Among South Central residents, the Campaign provided an opportunity for African Americans and Latino newcomers to work together for the first time. Both African Americans and Latinos attended the public meetings, which were conducted in English and Spanish. In neighborhoods like one known as "The Bottom," older African Americans walked door-to-door with young newcomer Mexican families in a successful effort to deny a "variance" to two liquor stores seeking to build in a residential zone. For hearings, the Coalition would provide transportation so both African Americans and Latino newcomers could testify. "Many of the African Americans had never known what the Spanish speakers felt about the community," says Castillo. "The hearings started some of the deepest friendships I've seen in a long time."

RESULTS AND NEXT STEPS

The Campaign's 17-month existence kept South Central residents active in what continues to be a long and difficult controversy. While legal battles dragged on, and a bitter and ugly public debate raged, the Campaign worked to encourage thoughtful, collective problem-solving among South Central's diverse residents. Although the Campaign could not hope to end the complex race and ethnic tensions emerging from South Central, it could try to minimize their negative impact. Castillo is proud, for example, that the Campaign helped neutralize support for a boycott of Korean stores. The Campaign's grassroots presence also had an important impact on local public policy, such as the decision to waive fees that discouraged liquor store owners from converting to other forms of business. The end of the Campaign also marked the beginning of a new effort called "Neighborhoods Fighting Back," which Castillo hopes will build on the past years' energy in addressing South Central's many urgent challenges.

COALITION STRUGGLES TO MEND DIVIDED NEIGHBORHOOD

CHICAGO, IL — Carmak Road, a busy four-lane thoroughfare, cuts a concrete gash between North and South Lawndale. To the north, African Americans dominate an area where years of factory closings have forced many residents to move. To the south, Mexican newcomers are pumping new energy into the long-standing Latino area of "Little Village." North and South Lawndale residents seldom interact, except on the shared turf of Faragut High School. In 1991 efforts to address tensions at Faragut produced the Lawndale Coalition, the first neighborhood-based Latino/African American coalition in Chicago.

That year, a series of violent incidents between African American and Latino gangs shook the community. The Chicago Human Relations Commission stepped in to set up a special task force to help Faragut students, parents, and teachers vent emotions and cool down. However, people quickly realized that this immediate response to crisis would not be enough. If a divided community were to become whole, something bigger had to happen.

In September 1991 parents and community leaders from both North and South Lawndale met for the first time to forge something bigger. More than 30 people attended the first meeting, including concerned parents, and representatives from the school board, local religious organizations, the police department, the city council, and the community hospital. This meeting, and others that followed, culminated in the creation of the Lawndale Coalition. The mission of the Lawndale Coalition is to "promote better understanding between residents of different cultural backgrounds" and "actively foster meaningful and continuous relations by addressing areas such as public safety and intercultural education." The Coalition began by establishing Co-Chairs, one African American from North Lawndale and one Mexican American from South Lawndale, as well as creating committees to address three major cross-cutting issues: education, public safety, and recreation. "Our goal is a self-sustaining community organization that holds institutions accountable for their role in race relations," says Roberto Cornelio, the Chicago Human Relations Commission staff member who helped found the coalition. "We are creating a process from which communities can put forward unique needs with respect."

Over the course of three years, the Coalition has successfully initiated communication between groups that had never before talked to each other, generated positive media coverage of community projects, and worked proactively to prevent violent conditions from worsening. Nonetheless, participants continue to struggle to preserve the Coalition. Maintaining African American participation has been a major challenge. For African American residents, who see their neighborhoods in decline and struggle to hang on to the power and resources they have, the Coalition's mission may seem less than urgent, or even a bit threatening. Many Mexican newcomers see themselves as competing with the African Americans; some even believe the "solution" to inter-ethnic tensions is waiting until all African Americans have left the community.

As the Lawndale Coalition fights its uphill battle, small but important breakthroughs take place. Ester Lopez, Associate Director of Latino Youth, recalls the Coalition's first meeting, during which several African Americans charged Latinos with racism: "One of the first things we had to do was define racism, to see that each group had its biases and prejudices, but that neither had the institutional power to be 'racist.'"

LATINO ORGANIZATION STRUGGLES FOR RESPECT, UNDERSTANDING

LOS ANGELES, CA — For most Americans the name "Watts" conjures up visions of a Black ghetto in flames. While Watts still faces serious economic and social challenges, its population today is at least 25 percent Latino. Despite such demographic changes, only one Latino organization exists in the area: the Watts/ Century Latino Organization (WCLO). Before WCLO's creation in 1990, there were no institutions promoting Latino residents' participation in community decision making nor was there any structure to help address tensions between Watts' Mexican immigrant population and its native-born African American population.

WCLO began as a grassroots effort to ensure that Latinos had a voice in the city's redevelopment plans for Watts. City officials had printed information and held hearings on the redevelopment plans, but failed to reach out to Latinos or to provide oral interpretation for non-English speakers. Local activist Arturo Ybarra pulled concerned Latino residents together to translate information into Spanish and held a community meeting in which interpreters helped city officials present their plans. "To their surprise and our pleasure, it worked," chuckles Ybarra. "Latinos showed up and participated."

WCLO has gone on to tackle two priority issues: crime and intergroup relations. The organization has tried to address widely publicized incidents of African American gangs victimizing Latinos in two local housing projects. These efforts brought WCLO into collaboration with Fred Williams, an African American former gang member who now runs the Cross Colors Foundation, and Connie Rice, an African American attorney with the NAACP Legal Defense and Education Fund. This alliance has resulted in unprecedented efforts — like a meeting of about 100 African American gang members and 50 Latinos — to try to diffuse tensions. WCLO also holds an annual Latino/African American Cinco de Mayo Festival, which brings together a broad range of community organizations.

WCLO plays a critical role in the Watts community, but still struggles to survive. WCLO has no paid staff and receives only tiny foundation grants for activities; community residents who want to get involved are often limited by the demands of work and childcare. Ybarra believes that newcomers can contribute to rebuilding the community with the help of strong institutions and innovations like stipends for community members whose finances prevent them from taking leadership responsibilities. Without resources, Ybarra argues, no one should be surprised that there are problems: "To make a difference, we need a team of people committed eight hours a day. We have to make that kind of investment."

LATINO MOTHERS SEEK COMMUNITY-WIDE PEACE

LOS ANGELES, CA — It's Friday night. A group of women walk past the cinder block walls of the Aliso Gardens housing project. Young men cluster around televisions in the courtyard, watching their idol, Julio Cesar Chavez, fight for the middleweight title. "Things are very quiet," the women whisper in Spanish, "because everyone's watching *el boxeo*." One woman nods toward a boy. "That's what my son looked like," she whispers, "until he got shot by the gangs."

These women are members of *Comite Pro Paz* (Committee for Peace), a Boyle Heights community group founded by mothers seeking an end to gang violence. The majority of Boyle Heights residents are Latino. Nonetheless, *Comite's* structure and activities reflect a remarkable level of diversity. The group itself includes white and African American women, while *Comite's* community activities provide a structured, positive way for African Americans and Latino newcomers to interact and work together.

Comite began four years ago as a project of Delores Mission, one of the oldest community institutions in Los Angeles. *Comite* wanted to stop the drug and turf wars that were leaving so many young people dead in the streets. But *Comite* members believed that the tough, sometimes brutal tactics of the local police were only making the young people more hostile and less likely to act responsibly. Rosa, one of the group's original members, explains in Spanish: "We wanted our children to feel respected as human beings. We realized we were afraid of our children, but that we were the only ones who could change the situation."

Comite began with walks around the neighborhood in which members would approach young men on the street and simply ask them about their concerns. What they found were not hardened criminals, but kids who wanted jobs, somewhere to play sports, and schools that were dedicated to educating them. *Comite* then began sponsoring barbecues where young people could get a meal and a chance to talk. *Comite's* first big event was a 1990 march against guns that drew nearly 1,000 local residents. *Comite* members went door-to-door asking the mothers and families of gang members to search for guns in their homes and then march to a garbage dumpster to throw the guns away. *Comite* members also organized a march on local factories demanding that they hire local youth. Although the factories did not respond, the press coverage caught the eye of a factory owner outside the area, who decided to offer jobs to a number of Boyle Heights youths.

Comite continues to thrive on the commitment and energy of its members, and gets by financially on small grants from sources like the Liberty Hill Foundation and the Campaign for Human Development, and proceeds from bake sales. "We need money for technical assistance," says Rosa, "to give us more structure, more strength, more power." Rosa also hopes *Comite* will be able to reach out beyond Latinos. "The Rodney King beating was a big injustice for all of us," says Rosa. "We've got to work together if things are going to change."

JEWS AND KOREANS TACKLE HEALTH CARE REFORM

NEW YORK, NY — Over the last two decades, thousands of Koreans have come to settle in the Flushing section of northern Brooklyn. Koreans now make up at least half of Flushing's population and have established solid community institutions like the Korean YWCA. Despite the presence of more established Jewish residents and Latin American newcomers, the Korean Y has remained focused on meeting the pressing needs of its own community. Now, thanks to the innovative efforts of the Jewish Community Relations Council (JCRC), the Korean Y has begun working with local Jewish organizations to ensure that the whole community's health care needs are met. According to Christy Kim of the Korean Y, "This is the first time these two groups are getting together and trying to do something concrete, not just talk."

Robert Kaplan, who directs JCRC's new Intergroup Relations and Community Concerns division, has been Flushing's Neighborhood-Based Health Coalition. "This is part of a whole new approach for us," says Kaplan. "The [racial violence] incidents in Crown Heights really taught us a lesson. We had to take a hard look at how we operated. We had no grassroots understanding of what to do." With funding from the United Jewish Appeal-Federation, the JCRC launched a community-based effort to strengthen relations between the Jewish community and the various ethnic, racial, and religious groups in the New York metropolitan area. As Kaplan began to tackle this effort he came to the conclusion that "Jews are living more and more with recent immigrants. Do we just live with it, or do we try to focus on improving the quality of life in these areas?"

While the JCRC's effort is just beginning, it may provide important lessons for other organizations. In Flushing, a jointly-sponsored Korean/Jewish forum on community health care issues recently attracted a diverse crowd of more than 200 participants. But if Kaplan is ambitious, he is also humble. "Our approach is to use what we know about dialogue and mediation as tools," he says. "No one has *the* answer."

COMMUNITY INNOVATIONS:

CITY-WIDE ADVOCACY

COALITION SEEKS ADULT EDUCATION FOR ALL

CHICAGO, IL — By the time the Adult Education Reform Coalition (AERC) was started in 1992, changes in Chicago's adult education system were long overdue. The educational system was in disarray, running a $10 million deficit and lacking any real leadership. Ignoring the advice of educators, economists, and business leaders, the system made little investment in adult education, which serves as a lifeline to newcomers learning English and to native Chicagoans seeking the basic skills employers require. More than half of all City College students were enrolled in adult education programs in 1990, but the system spent only 15 percent of its budget on them. Studies of the City College system found that it provided benefits — like guidance counseling, a range of classes and schedules, and clearly defined academic programs — to students in college-level courses, but not to adult education students.

Organizations representing different races and ethnicities had sought reform for years. However, the needs of each group were so urgent that advocates had little time to press for cross-cutting, system-wide change. By 1992, some advocates had grown tired of piecemeal strategies, and many were outraged by the City College Chancellor's plans to "streamline" the troubled adult education system by cancelling over 500 classes and closing community-based literacy programs. Unless advocates could forge a broad and unified opposition, the plan was likely to become a harsh reality. The Adult Education Reform Coalition hoped it could create that opposition, as well as a voice for positive change.

The AERC grew from the efforts of several committed advocates, such as Marta White, an African American woman from the Chicago Community Trust, and Nadja Papillon, a Haitian immigrant and former city college administrator. These advocates needed guidance, meeting space, and support to get started. So they turned to Travelers and Immigrants Aid (TIA) of Chicago, a local social service and advocacy agency with a reputation for working with both newcomers and established residents.

The fledgling AERC reached out to as many different groups as it could. Organizers were delighted when over 20 different organizations showed up for the first meeting. Because the meeting participants came from different racial and ethnic groups as well as different areas of the city, and because most had never worked together, perspectives and priorities sometimes clashed. "Airing conflict was key to helping the coalition stay alive in the beginning," recalls Papillon. "People expressed themselves. You can't ignore potential conflict points. You need to deal with them right away." In the end, the meeting participants agreed to work toward the creation of a high-quality adult education system that would build on the networks and expertise of local community organizations. AERC then received funding from the MacArthur Foundation to formalize itself. The Coalition staff grew to include a Mexican-born director and an African American community organizer.

The Coalition has had an important impact at a critical time. Its first achievement was to open up what had been a closed process for selecting a new City College Chancellor. In response to pressure from the Coalition, the search committee was expanded to include community representatives whose perspective ultimately shaped the final selection. The Coalition also managed to slow down the City College's plan to eliminate hundreds of community-based adult education classes as part of a "site consolidation" process. At first, the City College began eliminating different community-based sites without giving communities a chance to make the case for keeping them open. The Coalition was able to strike an agreement with the Chancellor that would allow it to participate in deciding which sites should close and on what basis. The Coalition's work helped decrease the number of sites that would close and saved approximately 5,000 adult students from losing their classes. The Coalition also led the effort to get a city council resolution to put a freeze on site closings and require the City College to address the needs of underserved communities.

COLLABORATIVE APPROACH TAKES TIME

LOS ANGELES, CA — When Los Angeles erupted in fire in April of 1992, racial and ethnic tensions became a crisis for city residents and Americans across the country. The chaos crashed in on many lives, including those of Joe Hicks and Stewart Kwoh. Hicks, head of the predominantly African American Southern Christian Leadership Conference (SCLC) of LA, and Kwoh, director of the Asian Pacific Law Caucus (APLC), were profoundly shaken by the violence, by the racial and ethnic hatred it expressed, and by their own inability to stop it. The two men became convinced that something new had to be created to address the urgent needs of African American, Latino, and Asian communities, and to turn tensions between them into a united force for change.

Hicks and Kwoh became the driving force behind the creation of the Los Angeles Multicultural Collaborative (MCC). The MCC, a coalition of organizations representing diverse communities, set out to build a new "human relations infrastructure" that would make intergroup organizing possible. The burning question for the MCC members was what they could do to be proactive, not just reactive. The twelve original MCC members, which included organizations like the Central American Resource Center (CARECEN), the Korean Youth and Community Center (KYCC), and the NAACP Legal Defense Fund, began with three observations. They believed that current approaches to human relations were not adequate, that organizations had developed effective ways of working together on policy issues and that grassroots support for such collaboration was lacking.

The MCC began by trying to assess human relations efforts that were already taking place in Los Angeles and making recommendations about what was needed. MCC's priorities have included stimulating ideas and plans for using economic development to improve communities and reduce intergroup tensions as well as developing and advocating ways to foster intergroup collaboration through the public education system. The fact that the MCC still exists, despite the logistical, financial, and political challenges it has faced, has also been a great accomplishment.

In the two years since its founding, the MCC has beaten the odds to preserve a vision and structure for multiethnic collaboration. In the immediate aftermath of the 1992 disturbances, many political leaders, members of the media, and individuals proclaimed the urgent need to revitalize urban economies and build solid relationships between different racial and ethnic groups. But other issues quickly captured the spotlight, leaving innovations like the MCC in the shadows. At the same time, the problems facing inner city African Americans, Latinos, and Asians often seemed too immediate and too overwhelming to allow time for intergroup cooperation. As Gary Phillips, one of three MCC Co-Directors observes, "It's very difficult to advance an agenda that's not at the forefront of the community. Intergroup collaboration can seem too esoteric."

WHAT HAVE WE LEARNED?

The National Immigration Forum undertook this project to learn how to build community efforts in which newcomers and established residents could work together for the benefit of all. While each of the stories included in this report has its own unique features and circumstances, we nonetheless identified some common themes among them. The following section discusses these themes as well as our conclusions about how to strengthen and promote such initiatives.

OBSERVATIONS: WHAT DO THESE EFFORTS TEACH US?

We have made four general observations based on the initiatives described in this report:

1) NEWCOMER/ESTABLISHED RESIDENT COLLABORATIONS CAN BE AN INSPIRING, INSTRUCTIVE, AND STRATEGIC PART OF REBUILDING AMERICAN COMMUNITIES.

Interaction between newcomers and established residents broadens the perspective of people in both groups, allows each to learn from the expertise and skills of the other, and increases the odds of improving the quality of life for all:

The initiatives we examined needed a concrete goal to motivate people to participate. They also needed a conscientious, explicit commitment to building good relationships within their community.

- An African American literacy teacher told us how working with newcomer women from Mexico had helped African American women gain the confidence and curiosity to go outside their neighborhood and seek new opportunities;
- An orthodox Jewish organization told us how its small business expertise and networks were guiding newcomer entrepreneurs and creating new jobs;
- A coalition of groups representing African Americans and Latino newcomers showed us how broad-based concern is promoting system-wide reforms in adult education.

The report also illustrates how newcomer/established resident initiatives can help neutralize deliberate attempts to foster divisiveness and hostility between groups.

2) HAVING A CONCRETE GOAL AND A COMMITMENT TO GOOD RELATIONS MAKES THESE INITIATIVES STRONGER AND MORE EFFECTIVE.

The initiatives we examined needed a concrete goal to motivate people to participate. They also needed a conscientious, explicit commitment to building good relationships within their community. For example, Chicago's Organization of the NorthEast became a community force by blending efforts to build personal relationships and cultural awareness between groups with an explicit, practical agenda for change.

A DESIRE FOR POSITIVE RELATIONS ALONE MAY NOT BE ENOUGH. The project indicates that a desire for "positive relations" or "reduced tensions" may not provide enough incentive for people to work together. Many of the people interviewed commented that even though they valued their interaction with people of different races, ethnicities, and national origins, they remained involved because of the immediacy and specificity of the initiative's goal.[32]

A CONCRETE GOAL ALONE MAY NOT IMPROVE RELATIONS. These findings suggest that a concrete goal *alone* will not ensure that new collaborative relationships take hold. This point was most evident among initiatives which set out to achieve a certain goal, leaving interaction among diverse participants to happen "naturally." Many of these initiatives ran into conflicts that forced participants to establish deliberate strategies for building good relations. The strategies included dialogue, mediation, and dispute resolution undertaken *in the context of the larger goal.* For example, in Los Angeles, Casa Loma took a laissez-faire approach to relations among the diverse housing development residents — then decided to set up conflict resolution training when tensions arose.

The Community Innovations findings echo those of the earlier Changing Relations project, which found that efforts to improve newcomer/established resident relations were more likely to be successful if they focused on a specific collaborative project. The Community Innovations findings are also consistent with a recent study of African American/Korean tensions which concluded that approaches to newcomer/established resident tensions must address individual attitudes and behavior *and* the political/economic situation in which people live.[33]

3) THESE COLLABORATIONS MADE A SERIOUS INVESTMENT IN "PROCESS."

In virtually every case, the "mundane" process of talking with participants, pulling them together, and keeping them informed took the most time and had the biggest impact on what the participants accomplished and the relationships they built. These initiatives depend on people committed to the processes that enable people to work together. Such people can separate themselves from the content of an initiative and focus on *how* something gets done:

■ The health reform collaboration between Korean newcomers and Jewish residents in New York depended on one organizer's ability and willingness to spend time finding out which barriers (such as schedule and custom) could limit each group's participation.

■ In Chicago's International Homes project, the staff of Voice of the People realized the need to respect the diverse steering committee's pace and information needs and to avoid treating them as "tokens."

PARTICIPATION V. ANALYSIS. The people in these initiatives we studied sought to understand different groups and draw them in through on-going participation. They focused on identifying and addressing the barriers that would make it difficult for certain groups to participate, and tried to remain critical of how the structure and practices of the initiative itself were helping or hindering participation. This approach differs from that of some "diversity training" programs that focus on analyzing cultural characteristics. As Gary Delgado describes in his recent assessment of prejudice reduction efforts, training is needed that does not "ignore the subjective questions of how people feel about themselves, but places greater emphasis on the degree to which organizational activities move people toward the goal of racial equality."[34]

Many of the people interviewed commented that even though they valued their interaction with people of different races, ethnicities, and national origins, they remained involved because of the immediacy and specificity of the initiative's goal.

COLLABORATIVE LEADERSHIP. The leadership of the initiatives we examined were committed to broad participation. Unlike the traditional notion of a "charismatic leader" who trailblazes visibly ahead of the flock, the leadership of the best initiatives, who were often people of color and people with a history in the community, often worked collaboratively and behind the scenes. Most had some organizing experience and/or training before they became involved:

■ The co-founder of the Central Brooklyn Credit Union grew up in the neighborhood and is the son of Jamaican immigrants; his formal leadership position evolved from his effort to pull diverse organizations together around the need for economic power.

■ The Campaign Against Problem Liquor Stores was headed by a second-generation Mexican American woman whose organizing experience began when she was a nurse mobilizing other nurses to become activists on community health issues.

AIRING CONFLICT. People interviewed in this project often described how much the initiative was strengthened by an honest and well-facilitated airing of conflicts between groups. Time and again, participants stressed the need for individuals and groups to have a chance to air their views and vent their emotions in a frank but constructive process. Participants believed that without such a process, sentiments could fester and ultimately destroy a collaboration.

INNOVATIVE REPRESENTATION AND PARTICIPATION. Intergroup initiatives must be built on an understanding of which institutions are important and specific to particular communities, and must develop appropriate ways for groups to represent themselves and participate in the initiative. For example, newcomers may not yet have developed organizations through which they can communicate their views, advocate on issues, or participate in coalitions. In Los Angeles, the Casa Loma project wanted its planning to include local newcomer Latinas, who were largely unorganized and often uncomfortable challenging "experts" like architects and lawyers. Casa Loma therefore brought together women from the community to participate in closed group discussions.

Poor quality interpretation not only discourages newcomers from participating, but established residents as well.

Marginalized groups such as low-income African Americans also need innovative and appropriate outreach. For example, the International Homes project chose to invite an African American church to participate in its next project because there were no African American institutions parallel to the newcomer mutual assistance associations (MAAs).

Getting different groups involved also means acknowledging differences in work schedules and family structure among different groups. For example, Justice for Janitors and WISH both struggled to schedule meetings that African Americans and Latino newcomers could attend together. It was difficult: the Latino newcomers were more likely to have young children and hold jobs at odd hours.

ORAL INTERPRETATION. Communication among members of different racial, ethnic, and national origin groups is a critical part of these processes. Poor quality interpretation (oral "translation") not only discourages newcomers from participating, but established residents as well. In areas with high numbers of newcomers, meetings may be held in a language other than English, meaning that English-speaking established residents may be shut out or discouraged by poor interpretation.

Virtually every initiative struggled with limited resources to provide interpretation (oral "translation") into various languages during meetings. While any effort at interpretation seemed to help, the quality of the efforts varied widely:

- In some cases, an interpreter would provide an incomplete or even inaccurate summary of an important discussion;
- Sometimes an interpreter would turn a provocative and inspiring speech into a dull, distracted monologue;
- Most often, interpretation was only provided for the "featured" speakers, not for discussion or for participants' questions.

One hopeful sign: the tiny fraction of initiatives which had the opportunity to use new headset technology were able to provide effective simultaneous interpretation.

4) STRONG NEWCOMER/ESTABLISHED RESIDENT INITIATIVES COMPLEMENT, RATHER THAN REPLACE, ORGANIZATIONS THAT REPRESENT THE PEOPLE OF ONE RACE, ETHNICITY, OR NATIONAL ORIGIN.

Many of the most promising initiatives we studied saw themselves as complementing, rather than replacing, existing single-group organizations:

- When Casa Atzlan decided to reach out to African Americans, it retained its institutional focus on newcomers, but developed a joint project that added a new intergroup dimension to its work and to that of the African American organization with which it collaborated.
- Although the Business Outreach Center project was launched by an orthodox Jewish organization, the network itself is built on existing community organizations which added new collaborations to their work.

DIFFERENT GROUPS, DIFFERENT NEEDS. Although the initiatives described in this report pulled people from different racial and ethnic groups together, they often acknowledged that not all issues cut across all groups. People in these initiatives also commented that each group needs to have institutions that reinforce and celebrate its unique identity, even as it works in collaboration with others.

SEGREGATION, ISOLATION, AND SELF-INTEREST. People interviewed felt that the segregation and isolation of different groups and the lack of a collective definition of self-interest made intergroup efforts an uphill struggle. Individuals in initiatives felt that until the public supports and acknowledges such efforts, people will have no proof of their effectiveness and will consider them a luxury at best and a diversion at worst.

These comments parallel those of activist and Stanford law professor Bill Ong Hing. Hing argues that, historically, the "rewards" for newcomer/established resident collaboration have been few.

> After decades, even centuries, of unsuccessfully trying to break into the social and political structures of the country, many [communities of color] concluded that they must take things into their own hands, forego reliance on the power structure, and look out for their own interests .... Their priority is taking care of themselves, since coalition work with other communities seems to have generated few rewards.[35]

CONCLUSIONS: WHAT DO NEWCOMER/ESTABLISHED RESIDENT EFFORTS NEED?

Our observations suggest a need to:

- Strengthen existing newcomer/established resident initiatives;
- Support existing organizations' ability to take on newcomer/established resident collaboration; and
- Stimulate the creation of new initiatives.

WHAT CAN WE DO?

As the previous chapter suggests, newcomer/established resident collaborations need many forms of support, including:

- **CONNECTING HUMAN RELATIONS AND OTHER COMMUNITY GOALS;**

- **ADEQUATE AND APPROPRIATE FINANCIAL SUPPORT;**

- **SPECIAL TRAINING AND TECHNICAL ASSISTANCE;**

- **A NEW WAY TO DOCUMENT SUCCESS;**

- **INCLUSIVE COMMUNITY PLANNING AND DECISION MAKING;**

- **OPPORTUNITIES TO MEET ORGANIZATIONS OUTSIDE THEIR TRADITIONAL NETWORK; AND**

- **ACCESS TO HIGH-QUALITY INTERPRETATION.**

Community organizations could seek new representatives for their boards, establish advisory committees that include new players, or develop experimental efforts such as focus groups.

This support can come from many sectors, including philanthropy, government, and local leadership. Following are specific ways to strengthen American communities by improving newcomer/established resident relations:

INCLUSIVE COMMUNITY PLANNING AND DECISION MAKING

- **FUNDERS SHOULD DEVELOP INNOVATIVE FUNDING STRATEGIES** that draw in new and underrepresented populations and help them define what their communities need. Examples to consider include the Community Bridges initiative of the Los Angeles Community Foundation and the Community Partnership initiative of the Arlington Community Foundation.

- **FUNDERS AND POLICY MAKERS SHOULD SUPPORT STUDIES THAT EXAMINE HOW SPECIFIC POLICIES AND PROGRAMS HURT OR HELP RELATIONS BETWEEN NEWCOMERS AND ESTABLISHED RESIDENTS.** They should also support studies of how some employers, landlords, and others may deliberately foster intergroup hostilities to their advantage, and how public policies could be crafted to stop such practices. One goal of these studies should be to demonstrate how much more the "costs" of responding to intergroup crises are compared with the benefits of investing in proactive community-building strategies.

- **POLICY MAKERS SHOULD EXAMINE WAYS TO INCLUDE REPRESENTATIVES OF MARGINALIZED GROUPS** — both newcomers and established residents — when deciding what kinds of programs and policies are needed, and by whom.

- **POLICY MAKERS SHOULD DRAW PUBLIC ATTENTION TO THE NEED FOR NEWCOMER/ ESTABLISHED RESIDENT COLLABORATION** by holding hearings on related issues and community and public policy responses.

- **COMMUNITY ORGANIZATIONS SHOULD FIND WAYS TO OBTAIN INPUT FROM DIFFERENT COMMUNITY MEMBERS.** This could mean seeking new representatives for their boards, establishing advisory committees that include new players in the development of an innovative project, or developing "experimental" efforts, such as focus group discussions.

- **COMMUNITY ORGANIZATIONS SHOULD EXAMINE WAYS TO WORK WITH FUNDERS AND POLICY MAKERS IN GATHERING INFORMATION,** perhaps seeking funds to conduct local surveys or focus groups, or collaborating with a nearby university.

CONNECTING HUMAN RELATIONS AND OTHER COMMUNITY GOALS

- **FUNDERS AND POLICY MAKERS SHOULD SEEK WAYS TO INCORPORATE THE GOAL OF IMPROVED RELATIONS INTO EXISTING FUNDING CATEGORIES, PROGRAMS, AND POLICIES.** As long as race and ethnic relations remain ghettoized in an isolated funding category, intergroup relations will lack the community context that gives them meaning. Work in other arenas, such as economic development, housing, and community organizing, will also suffer from the lack of a strategic understanding of intergroup relations.

- **COMMUNITY ORGANIZATIONS SHOULD EXPLORE WAYS IN WHICH THEIR MISSION, GOALS, AND OBJECTIVES WOULD COMPLEMENT OR BENEFIT FROM AN INTERGROUP INITIATIVE.**

ADEQUATE AND APPROPRIATE FUNDING

- **FUNDERS AND POLICY MAKERS SHOULD PROVIDE GENERAL SUPPORT FUNDING TO EXISTING INTERGROUP EFFORTS.** As they do this, they should be careful not to create competition for funding between single-group and intergroup efforts.

- **FUNDERS AND POLICY MAKERS SHOULD PROVIDE FUNDS TO HELP INFORMAL INTERGROUP EFFORTS MAKE THE TRANSITION INTO PERMANENT INITIATIVES.** Without funding, such efforts have little chance of long-term survival.

- **FUNDERS AND POLICY MAKERS SHOULD PROVIDE CORE SUPPORT FUNDING FOR SINGLE- GROUP EFFORTS AND ENCOURAGE THEIR INTERACTION WITH OTHER GROUPS** by providing them with additional funds specifically targeted for intergroup work. Single-group organizations should not be forced to sacrifice their core work in order to do intergroup work.

SPECIAL TRAINING AND TECHNICAL ASSISTANCE

■ **FUNDERS AND POLICY MAKERS SHOULD PROVIDE FUNDING TO CREATE AND SUPPORT TRAINING AND TECHNICAL ASSISTANCE PROGRAMS THAT HELP COMMUNITIES DEVELOP NEWCOMER/ESTABLISHED RESIDENT INITIATIVES** that address both human relations and other community goals. Funders and policy makers should also provide community organizations with funding to secure such training and technical assistance.

A NEW WAY TO DOCUMENT SUCCESS

■ **FUNDERS AND POLICY MAKERS MUST FIND WAYS TO MEASURE THE EFFECTIVENESS OF HUMAN RELATIONS WORK.** These measures should assess how an organization works through and with others, in addition to other measures that may assess how many people an organization "serves." The definitions and criteria used in this project may serve as a useful guide. For example, such assessment could measure evidence of strong community participation, such as meeting attendance and volunteer hours contributed.

Single-group organizations should not be forced to sacrifice their core work in order to do intergroup work.

■ **COMMUNITY ORGANIZATIONS CAN INFLUENCE FUNDERS AND POLICY MAKERS BY DESIGNING PROGRAMS AND FUNDING PROPOSALS WITH MEASURABLE INTERGROUP OBJECTIVES.** Community organizations can help redefine "effectiveness" by introducing practical measures for themselves and those assessing them.

■ **COMMUNITY ORGANIZATIONS CAN HELP CHANGE COMMUNITY EXPECTATIONS BY SPEAKING OUT AGAINST POLICIES AND PROGRAMS THAT HAVE A NEGATIVE IMPACT ON INTERGROUP RELATIONS.**

NEW NETWORK OPPORTUNITIES

■ **FUNDERS SHOULD CONVENE FORUMS AND MEETINGS IN WHICH REPRESENTATIVES OF DIFFERENT RACIAL, ETHNIC, AND NATIONAL ORIGIN GROUPS DISCUSS OVERARCHING CONCERNS.** Philanthropists should introduce different leaders and organizations who are addressing similar concerns in different groups.

■ **COMMUNITY ORGANIZATIONS SHOULD COMMIT TO IDENTIFYING AND MEETING WITH AT LEAST ONE COMMUNITY LEADER OR PROGRAM DIRECTOR FROM A RACIAL, ETHNIC, OR NATIONAL ORIGIN GROUP WITH WHICH THEY ARE NOT YET FAMILIAR.**

ACCESS TO HIGH-QUALITY INTERPRETATION

■ **FUNDERS AND POLICY MAKERS SHOULD PROVIDE FUNDING TO MAKE INTERPRETATION AND TRANSLATION SERVICES AND EQUIPMENT AVAILABLE** to community organizations and to improve the quality and availability of interpretation services.

■ **COMMUNITY ORGANIZATIONS SHOULD SEEK WAYS TO PROVIDE LANGUAGE INTERPRETATION AND TRANSLATION OR EXAMINE WAYS TO IMPROVE THE QUALITY OF CURRENT SERVICES.**

ENDNOTES

1. Cornel West, *Race Matters* (New York: Vintage Books, 1994), 159.

2. Ellis Cose, *A Nation of Strangers: Prejudice, Politics, and the Populating of America* (New York: William Morrow, 1992), 32.

3. John W. Gardner, *Building Community* (Washington, DC: Independent Sector, 1991), 15.

4. For a detailed description of the project methodology see page 15.

5. Robert L. Bach, *Changing Relations: Newcomers and Established Residents in U.S. Communities* (New York: Ford Foundation, 1993). *Copies may be obtained through the Ford Foundation.*

6. Ibid.

7. Anna Deavere Smith, *Fires in the Mirror: Crown Heights, Brooklyn and Other Identities* (New York: Anchor Books, 1993), xli.

8. For a listing of Advisory Committee members see page 92.

9. The National Conference of Christians and Jews, *Taking America's Pulse: A Summary Report of the National Conference Survey on Inter–Group Relations* (New York: National Conference of Christians and Jews, 1993), 10.

10. Henry G. Cisneros, "Social Contract for the Year 2000: Diversity As An Asset" (speech delivered before the National Civic League's 98th National Conference on Diversity, Los Angeles, November 1992), 3.

11. James Baldwin, *The Fire Next Time* (New York: Dial Press, 1963).

12. Michael Fix and Jeffrey S. Passel, *Immigration and Immigrants: Setting the Record Straight* (Washington, DC: Urban Institute, 1994), 29.

13. Barry Edmonston and Jeffrey S. Passel, eds., *Immigration and Ethnicity: The Integration of America's Newest Arrivals* (Washington, DC: Urban Institute, 1994), 13.

14. According to New York University professor Walter Stafford, "the 1993 *United Nations Human Development Report* [finds that] the social and economic conditions of African Americans and Latinos in the United States are significantly worse than in some of the countries the immigrants left."

15. Fix and Passel, *Setting the Record Straight*, 5.

16. Rudolph W. Giuliani, (opening remarks at the U.S. Commission on Civil Rights hearing "Racial & Ethnic Tensions in American Communities: Poverty, Inequality & Discrimination," U.S. Court of International Trade, September 1994), 1.

17. Joseph J. Salvo and Ronald J. Ortiz, *The Newest New Yorkers: An Analysis of Immigration into New York City During the 1980s* (New York: New York Department of City Planning, 1992), 2.

18. Ibid., 4.

19. Mike Davis, *City of Quartz* (New York: Vintage Books, 1992), 6.

20. Bureau of the Census, *Supplementary Reports on Urbanized Areas of the U.S. and Puerto Rico* (Washington, DC: U.S. Department of Commerce, 1990).

21. Paul M. Ong and Janette R. Lawrence, *Pluralism and Residential Patterns in Los Angeles* (Los Angeles: University of California, 1992), 27.

22. Iris J. Lav, Edward B. Lazere, and Jim St. George, *A Tale of Two Futures: Restructuring California's Finances to Boost Economic Growth* (Washington, DC: Center on Budget and Policy Priorities, 1994), vii.

23. Amy Teschner, ed., *Sweet Home Chicago: The Real City Guide* (Chicago: Chicago Review Press, 1993), 17.

24. The Chicago Community Trust, "Common Differences: Chicago's Immigrant Experience," *Chicago Sun Times*, June 14, 1994, Supplement.

25. Amy Teschner, ed., *Sweet Home Chicago*, 17.

26. Katherine Boo, "Washington: Divided, Even Where the Races Meet," *The Washington Post*, October 21, 1994, sec. A16.

27. Robert D. Manning and David E. Pedersen, *Six Months Later—Multicultural Washington, D.C.: The Changing "Complexion" of Social Inequality* (Washington, DC: The American University, 1992).

28. Metropolitan Washington Council of Governments, *Population Change in Metropolitan Washington: A Comparison of 1980 and 1990 Census Data by Age, Race, Sex, and Ethnic Group*, Table 3, Washington, DC, August, 1991.

29. Arnold & Porter, *Immigration Law: A Civil Rights Issue—The Human Impact of Immigration and Refugee Law on the District of Columbia's Latino Population* (Washington, DC: Washington Lawyer's Committee for Civil Rights under Law, 1992), 10.

30. Ibid., 139.

31. Patricia Orloff Grow et al., *Racial and Ethnic Tensions in American Communities: Poverty, Inequality, and Discrimination*, vol. 1, *The Mount Pleasant Report* (Washington, DC: U.S. Commission on Civil Rights, 1993), 139.

32. Our interviews with people involved in efforts *not* included in this report also suggest that efforts established *solely* to promote positive interaction or respond to a dramatic conflict may have difficulty keeping people engaged.

33. Lucie Cheng and Yen Espiritu, "Korean Businesses in Black and Hispanic Neighborhoods: A Study of Intergroup Relations," *Sociological Perspectives* 32, no. 4 (1989).

34. Gary Delgado, *Anti–Racist Work: An Examination and Assessment of Organizational Activity* (Oakland, Applied Research Center, 1992), 59.

35. Bill Ong Hing, "Beyond the Rhetoric of Assimilation and Cultural Pluralism: Addressing the Tension of Separatism and Conflict in an Immigration–Driven Multiracial Society," *California Law Review* 81, no. 4 (1993), 895.

How to Contact These Community Innovations

Adult Education Reform Coalition
c/o Travelers and
Immigrants Aid
208 South LaSalle Street
Room 1818
Chicago, IL 60604
(312) 629–4500

Alliance for Neighborhood Economic Development
3470 Wilshire Blvd.
Suite 1110
Los Angeles, CA 90010
(213) 365–7400

Barnabas Self Employment Fund
2712 Ontario Road, N.W.
Washington, DC 20009
(202) 667–8970

Business Outreach Network
c/o Council of
Jewish Organization
5524 13th Avenue
Brooklyn, NY 11219
(718) 436–1550

Campaign to Rebuild South Central Without Problem Liquor Stores
c/o Community Coalition for
Substance Abuse Prevention
8500 South Broadway
Los Angeles, CA 90003
(213) 750–9087

Casa Loma
379 S. Loma Drive
Los Angeles, CA 90017
(213) 484–9805

Central Brooklyn Federal Credit Union
1205 Fulton Street
Brooklyn, NY 11216–2004
(718) 399–1763

Comite Pro Paz
131 South Gless Street
Los Angeles, CA 90033
(213) 881–0024

Intercultural Family Literacy Program
c/o Casa Aztlan
1831 South Racine
Chicago, IL 60608
(312) 666–5508

International Homes Project
c/o Voice of the People
4753 North Broadway – #1010
Chicago, IL 60604
(312) 769–2442

Justice for Janitors – SEIU Local 82
1213 K Street, N.W.
3rd Floor
Washington, DC 20005
(202) 789–8282

Lawndale Coalition
c/o Commission on
Human Relations
City of Chicago
510 N Peshtigo Court
6th Floor
Chicago, IL 60611
(312) 744–4111

Leadership Development In Interethnic Relations (LDIR)
1010 South Flower Street
Room 302
Los Angeles, CA 90015
(213) 748–2022

LOS ANGELES MULTICULTURAL COLLABORATIVE (MCC)
1010 South Flower Street
Suite 211
Los Angeles, CA 90015
(213) 748–2105

NEIGHBORHOOD-BASED HEALTH COALITION
c/o Jewish Community
Relations Council (Flushing
Coalition)
711 Third Avenue
12th Floor
New York, NY 10017
(212) 983–4800

ORGANIZATION OF THE NORTHEAST (ONE)
5121 North Clark Street
Chicago, IL 60640
(312) 769–3232

SIDEWALK VENDING COALITION
1521 Wilshire Boulevard
Los Angeles, CA 90017
(213) 353–1346

TENANTS AND WORKERS SUPPORT COMMITTEE (TWSC)
3805 Mt. Vernon Avenue, #5
Alexandria, VA 22305
(703) 684–5697

WASHINGTON INNER CITY SELF HELP (WISH)
1419 V Street, NW
Washington, DC 20009
(202) 332–8800

WATTS/CENTURY LATINO ORGANIZATION (WCLO)
2214 East 108th Street
Los Angeles, CA 90059
(213) 564–9140

PROJECT ADVISORY COMMITTEE MEMBERS

ADVISORY COMMITTEE MEMBERS

Frank Acosta
Center for Community Change
Los Angeles, CA

Robert Bach, Senior Associate
Carnegie Endowment for International Peace
Washington, D.C.

Una Clark, New York Council Member
New York City Council
New York, NY

Gary Delgado, Executive Director
Applied Research Center
Oakland, CA

Barbara Huie, Chief of Planning and Evaluation
Department of Justice, Community Relations Services
Washington, D.C.

Bong Hwan Kim, Executive Director
Korean Youth & Community Center
Los Angeles, CA

Helen Lauffer, Director
Immigration and Homelessness Services
Traveler's Aid Service
New York, NY

Sid Mohn, Executive Director
Traveler's & Immigrants Aid of Chicago
Chicago, IL

Susan Jones, Instructor in Clinical Law
George Washington National Law Center
Washington, D.C.

Salim Muwakkil, Senior Editor
In These Times Magazine
Chicago, IL

Nestor Rodriguez, Associate Professor
University of Houston
Houston, TX

Yvonne Vega, Executive Director
AYUDA, Inc.
Washington, D.C.

Ronald Wakabayashi, Executive Director
Los Angeles County Human Relations Commission
Los Angeles, CA

For more information about the National Immigration Forum
and its activities, please write:

THE NATIONAL IMMIGRATION FORUM

220 I Street, NE

Suite 220

Washington, D.C. 20002